D0407168

APR 1 6 2008

DATE DUE			
9/30			

DOUBLE OR NOTHING

DOUBLE OR NOTHING

How Two Friends Risked It All to Buy
One of Las Vegas' Legendary Casinos

TOM BREITLING with CAL FUSSMAN

An Imprint of HarperCollinsPublishers

FIRST EDITION

Designed by Mary Austin Speaker

Library of Congress Cataloging-in-Publication Data
Breitling, Tom.
Double or nothing : how two friends risked it all to buy one of Las Vegas' legendary casinos / Tom Breitling and Cal Fussman.
    p.   cm.
  ISBN 978-0-06-083583-5
  1. Golden Nugget (Las Vegas, Nev.) 2. Casinos–Nevada–Las Vegas. I. Fussman, Cal. II. Title.
HV6711.B74 2008
338.7'617950922793135–dc22
[B]
        2007039065
08 09 10 11 12 OV/RRD 10 9 8 7 6 5 4 3 2 1

To Tim, an American original,
and the best friend a guy could ever hope for

CONTENTS

1   Holding Up The House   1

2   The Wise Guy   15

3   The Square   33

4   In-credible!   46

5   Are You Ready for This?   61

6   Smashing Through   76

7   Substance Is Everything   90

8   Who? Me? Tom Corleone?   104

9   Steve's Blessing   118

10 The Bait Is Too Strong   131

11 Fly Me to the Moon   145

12 Fifty-Foot Heads   158

13 Two Porterhouses and a Vegetarian   171

14 The Gambler   185

15 Project Goldfish   201

16 The Odds Couple   216

17 The Best of It   234

    Acknowledgments   239

DOUBLE OR NOTHING

CHAPTER 1

HOLDING UP THE HOUSE

"Royalty is coming."

Well, Johnny D. didn't say it exactly like that. Mr. Royalty is what we'll have to call a guy whose real name I can't tell you. The House doesn't reveal the identities of its gamblers. But Mr. Royalty is a good cover. There's plenty of truth and irony in it.

The truth is Mr. Royalty was able to swagger into The Golden Nugget carrying a pillowcase stuffed with hundred-dollar bills over his shoulder because of the royalties he was making off a line of video games that he'd created. If you're a man between eighteen and forty, you know his games. You've probably played them. One of his games grew so popular, rumor is he sold it outright for $40 million.

The irony in the name is that there's nothing regal about him. Even when he was winning millions at the craps table, he could be a five-alarm asshole. The dice never seem to come back to Mr. Royalty fast enough. "Gimme them!" he'd bark at the croupier. "Don't mess up my rhythm!" When he was losing, he'd abuse everyone around him—not even the cocktail waitresses were immune.

Mr. Royalty had been thrown out of quite a few casinos around Las Vegas. The owner of one hotel swore that even if he had a crystal ball showing Mr. Royalty losing $20 million at his casino over the next year, he still wouldn't let him through the doors. And my partner, Tim, was definitely conflicted about having Mr. Royalty at The Golden Nugget.

Tim has been described as a throwback—the oldest young man on the planet. Even though he was thirty-six and this was October 2004, he lived his life to the tunes of Frank Sinatra. That was one of the reasons Tim and I bought The Golden Nugget in the first place. We'd try to restore it to the glory of the Sinatra days and at the same time bring some color to a faded downtown.

Sinatra was now buried under a tombstone inscribed with the title of one of our favorite songs: "The Best Is Yet to Come." But an old friend of Frank's was still around. So we'd brought in Tony Bennett to sing at The Nugget. We had the cast of *The Sopranos* in our swimming pool. We set up a reality TV show around our casino with the same producer who'd made "You're Fired!" one of the most popular phrases in America. The idea was to create a buzz that would make people want to leave The Strip and take the twenty-minute drive downtown to be at The Nugget. Most of all, we wanted The Nugget to be *the* spot in Vegas to place a bet.

If every other casino was offering gamblers five times odds, Tim figured we'd give them ten. If your limit was $50,000 a hand at your hotel, Tim might let you play for $100,000 a hand at The Nugget. The strategy was pretty simple. We'd give you a better chance to win than anybody else and let you bet more.

When you throw that kind of chum into the water, you're going to attract sharks like Mr. Royalty. We didn't want his profanity, but we sure wanted his pillowcase. And more than that—we wanted the action.

We wanted people to tell their friends how Mr. Royalty had come with stacks of hundred-dollar bills that had been wrapped in plastic, vacuum sealed, and trucked direct from the U.S. Mint. When other high rollers got a whiff of mint in the air, they'd want in on the action, too. There are less than a hundred gamblers in the world with more than a million-dollar credit line. At one point, four of them came to visit us on a single weekend.

There was only one problem. We were gambling. We were still building up our clientele. And we needed a few others betting like Mr. Royalty that night in order to make the percentages work for us. The numbers were still in our favor—even with the special odds Tim was cutting Mr. Royalty. But we wouldn't have to sweat out a run of luck if others were betting big at the same time. Because then, even if Mr. Royalty did win big, percentages pretty much guarantee that together the others would lose at least enough to balance the books.

So we were vulnerable that night. We were vulnerable to one wild wave of luck.

And it just so happened that Mr. Royalty was on the Bonzai Pipeline.

He'd pulled up at The Nugget one night at the end of September in his $350,000 Maybach and six hours and three minutes later walked out with $4,753,200 of our money.

A week later he came back in for three and a half hours and took us for another $1.5 million. But let me give you an idea of how insane his touch had become. Before he even got to the dice pit, he sat down at a slot machine and hit a $100,000 jackpot.

Tim and I had taken the keys to The Nugget only ten months earlier. In less than ten hours, Mr. Royalty had basically wiped out what was going to be a great third-quarter profit. To us, that was more than just a figure on a spreadsheet. It was a number that told the world we weren't just a couple of kids who got lucky and hit the jackpot during the dot-com boom. It told the world we were entrepreneurs who knew how to make a business soar.

That number was now gone. The critics in the press who sneered whenever Tim and I took a risk that flopped would now have more ammo. And we didn't need Ed Borgato, the man who tracked our finances and who was eating dinner with us that night, to remind us that in two weeks we owed our investors a $7.5 million interest payment. But he did anyway.

There are few people in this world who believe in themselves more than Tim. What's that expression? Sometimes wrong, but never in doubt. Only now his eyes were puffy. The eighteen-hour workdays and the beating we'd opened ourselves up to by extending the high limits was taking a toll on both of us.

When Johnny D. came over to our table to alert us that Mr. Royalty was on his way over again, I felt my heart squeeze. I didn't know if this was the night we'd get it all back, or if the Bonzai Pipeline would turn into a tsunami.

It was nearing midnight. We'd been working since eight in the morning. Our day was just beginning.

I headed to the security room with Ed to watch on the surveillance cameras. Tim got up to greet our guest.

Mr. Royalty came through the doors with a small entourage like a fighter walking down an aisle of a packed arena to enter the ring. Didn't matter that his belly looked like he'd been training on Krispy Kremes. Dressed in sweats, he was bobbing and weaving with a cold-blooded snake-eye stare. There's a description for that sort of entrance in Vegas. He walked in, they say, like he wanted to change the name of the joint.

Johnny D. went to make sure Mr. Royalty's private table was just right. Right for Mr. Royalty, and right for The House. We needed dealers at that table who wouldn't be intimidated and a boxman with an iron bladder. On that table, one simple mistake on a dealer payout could cost us $100,000. And one of the many items on Mr. Royalty's list of requests was that the box man—the guy sitting at the center of the table responsible for all The House's chips—could not leave his seat even if he had to take a piss. These demands drove Tim crazy. "It's not his hotel! He does not make the rules!" But we wanted our money back. What could we do?

The chips were neatly stacked—yellows, whites, and blues. The yellows were $1,000. The whites were $5,000. The blues were $25,000. Mr. Royalty was putting up a million in cash to start.

Tim walked over. That was one of the things we prided ourselves on. There were hardly any casinos left in Vegas where the customers could meet the owners and have a conversation on the floor. People loved this. It made them feel special. It made them feel at home. It made them want to come back.

But the greeting between Tim and Mr. Royalty was a different sort of hello. "Hey, welcome back," didn't really mean "Good to see you." It was more like the ceremonial tapping of gloves by two boxers in the center of the ring—just before they tried to knock each other's brains out.

Maybe Tim knew it was going to be like this. I had no idea it would get this personal. But then, I'd never even seen what a hundred dollar bill looked like before I went to college.

I stood in the security room with my arms crossed staring

up at a wall filled with fifty flat-screened monitors. My eyes honed like lasers on Mr. Royalty's table. The security director, Randy, could maneuver the cameras so that Ed and I could see the action from four angles on different screens. No way could there be any funny business. Our cameras could zoom in and read the time off Mr. Royalty's watch.

Johnny D., our vice president of marketing, went to watch the monitors in his office. I didn't know where Tim was. But I knew he was watching. Not only were there monitors in his office, he'd had them installed in his home.

Maybe it was better that we were in different places. When we were side by side in front of the screens when a player like Mr. Royalty was winning, the tension crackled between us.

Craps can look complicated if you're approaching the table for the first time—especially if there are twenty people around it screaming their lungs out. But the game was stripped down at Mr. Royalty's table. He was the only one rolling.

The rules are fairly simple. If Mr. Royalty bets the pass line and his first roll of the two dice totals 7 or 11, he's a winner. There's only a 22 percent chance of that happening.

If Mr. Royalty's first roll totals a 2, 3, or 12, then we take Mr. Royalty's money. That will do him in 11 percent of the time.

If Mr. Royalty's first roll is 4, 5, 6, 8, 9, or 10, then that number will be Mr. Royalty's point. He'll have to roll his point again before he rolls a 7 in order to win. If he rolls a 7 before he rolls his point, he loses.

After Mr. Royalty makes a point, the odds are only slightly in our favor that he won't make his number, 51.3 percent. But once he begins to roll, the odds climb.

- 67 percent of the time, he'll roll a 7 and lose before rolling another 4.

- 60 percent of the time, he'll roll a 7 and lose before rolling another 5.
- 54 percent of the time, he'll roll a 7 and lose before rolling another 6.
- 54 percent of the time, he'll roll a 7 and lose before rolling another 8.
- 60 percent, he'll roll a 7 and lose before rolling another 9.
- 67 percent, he'll roll a 7 and lose before rolling another 10.

There are plenty of ways to bet. The roller can have up to a dozen bets going at one time. But the more he picks up the dice, the more the odds grind against him. Eventually, he'll be crushed.

Mr. Royalty scooped up the dice and shook them as if he could confuse them into forgetting that fact.

You know the feeling you get when a fighter you've bet on gets knocked down ten seconds into the fight? That ominous feeling? That the fates are against you, that the fight is already over before it even started?

Well then, you know the tension that spread through my gut when Mr. Royalty made his first point. He pumped his fists, and his entourage pumped with him. Then he reached out, swept in his winnings, and pushed out his bets. Right from the start, he was betting on himself in almost every possible way.

Mr. Royalty won his second roll, his third, and his fourth. A mountain of chips began to rise in front of his belly. He reached for the dice and won again.

I looked down at the floor. When you're in a fight, it's no good to look down.

"Call Johnny D.," I said to Randy. "See how much he's winning."

Mr. Royalty was filling the table with chips. Some bets he

was winning. Some bets he was losing. But the overall picture was not hard for a guy who'd been around the tables as long as Johnny D. to assess. "He's winning about $110,000 on every roll," he said.

In a couple of minutes, we were down more than half a million.

Half a million bucks, and we weren't even getting any atmosphere out of it. There's no better sound in a casino than twenty people around a craps table, slapping hands, hugging one another, and screaming "Open the suitcases!"

A scene like that makes anybody who's passed through the doors happy. Even our dealers are happy, because the winners are tossing them tips. We need that spirit in The House. Because quietly, all around, we're getting it back. People have to win. If nobody ever won, nobody would ever come back to Las Vegas.

But somehow Mr. Royalty had turned the tables on us. He was winning at a private table. The atmosphere around him was filled with profanity. And he'd been known to throw tips high in the air as if he were throwing a dog a bone—just to watch people jump for them. There was silence in the security room. A Led Zeppelin song coming out of a distant radio only seemed to magnify the tension.

Six wins in a row. Seven, eight, nine.

The sloppy mountain grew higher and wider. The mountain was what made Mr. Royalty scary. Most people stack their chips in neat piles. They like to know exactly how much they've got. They want to have their money near them, under their control, in a secure pile. Most people are not only scared to lose, Johnny D. will tell you. They're also scared to win.

Mr. Royalty was fearless. He wasn't holding anything back. Not only was he smart enough to know the exact value of all the chips in front of him, but he wanted them in play. A fearless gambler is the one who strikes fear in the heart of The House.

Ten in a row.

I felt my eyes close and my head shake. The odds of a roller winning ten straight at craps are 1,361-1.

Tim was born with the stomach for this. But I was still trying to develop some kind of lining. I knew about gamblers who were up $900,000, who were driven to beat The House for a million—and in the process lost it all. I'd seen million-dollar swings in a few hours. So I understood the concept of patience.

Patience is your best friend when you're The House. A bunch of kids from MIT might devise a system of counting cards on the blackjack tables, win $4 million, and make a name having a book written about it. But that's the exception. No gambler outlives the test of time. Time is always on the side of The House. So the idea is to master the art of time. When you've done so for decades like Steve Wynn, you can even afford to play with it.

There's a story Johnny D. likes to tell about a guy who cashed his Social Security check and went to play blackjack at Treasure Island. This was back in the day when Steve Wynn was running it. The guy had no shoes and only two teeth, and he ran his Social Security check up to more than $1.2 million. When Steve got word, he offered the guy a suite, tried to get him into the shower so the guy wouldn't offend the other players, and even offered him money for a book contract.

Steve knew he couldn't buy publicity like that. Guy cashes his Social Security check and turns it into a million bucks. Where? Treasure Island. The way Johnny D. tells it, Steve wanted the guy to stop right there.

Steve knew what was going to happen if he didn't cut the guy off. But the guy wouldn't settle up. "Who do you think you are, telling me to stop?" the guy shot back. "What are you, scared?"

It wasn't long before he'd lost it all.

Now, if Tim and I owned a large corporation that had a fleet of hotels, we might learn how to exercise that kind of influence. The million that Mr. Royalty had taken from us in less than an hour would be meaningless. Money would be surging into our business through celebrity-chef restaurants, the sale of jewels, designer clothes, and hundreds of other sources.

But Tim and I weren't a big corporation. We were two guys standing up to the pounding of Mr. Royalty's luck—and the worst part about the beating was it was splitting us apart.

We'd become so close over the years we could finish each other's sentences. But after Mr. Royalty had started on his tear, I didn't even have to open my mouth. "I know, Tom, I know," Tim would say before I could even get a word out.

Eleven in a row. Twelve. Thirteen.

As hard as it was to take, it was hard to argue with Tim. The casino was his world—not mine. And I certainly understood his thinking.

"Look, Tom," he explained. "The odds are on our side, and nobody beats the math. All I know is he'll blow the money. It may not be today. It may not be tomorrow. It may not be next week. But in time, he *will* blow the money. And he won't blow it at The Nugget if we don't let him play. We've got the best of it. And if we've got the best of it, why take a small shot? If I think I'm getting the best of it, hey, I'm betting as much as I can. It's a ballsy proposition here. It's gonna be a roller coaster ride. But we don't have a public company to answer to. It's just you and me. As long as we can pay our interest payments, who gives a shit? In the long run, we'll get all the money. In the short run, we'll just have to hold onto our balls and stick it out. We just have to keep him at the table."

Fourteen in a row. Fifteen.

The yellow, white, and blue mountain climbed over Mr. Royalty's belly. How much longer could this go on? How much longer could we let it go on with more than a hundred thousand on each roll?

Sixteen. Seventeen. Eighteen.

I felt like I was going to puke.

Nineteen. Twenty.

Twenty-one.

What the . . . ?

The odds of a roller at craps going twenty-two straight are 7,869,881-1

Sonavabitch!

On the twenty-third roll, Mr. Royalty crapped out. Even accounting for his losing bets on the last roll, he had to be up more than two million. But now that his streak had been broken, maybe luck would start to swing our way.

I stared at the monitors. What was going on? Mr. Royalty was no longer asking for the dice. He wanted to cash out.

I was too stunned to think. Wherever he was, Tim had to be going crazy. When you're The House, there's only one thing worse than losing like that: That's wondering if the guy who just beat you out of two million bucks will leave and head straight for another casino—where he'll proceed to lose *your* money.

Mr. Royalty walked over to the cage to collect. He'd come into the casino with cash wrapped in plastic directly from the U.S. Mint. And he wanted to leave with money wrapped by the U.S. Mint.

Johnny D. met him at the cage and watched as two Golden Nugget shopping bags were filled with green bricks.

We always monitored our big players as they headed out the doors. We needed to make sure there were no hiccups. We needed to make sure that Mr. Royalty wasn't confronted on the way out by anybody who'd watched him rake in the chips. We wanted to make sure the doormen and valet parkers treated him well. And we wanted to get an idea if he was headed to another casino or driving toward home.

We watched Mr. Royalty walk out the door. As Johnny D. would say, "Got his load and hit the road."

In less than two weeks, Mr. Royalty had beaten us for nearly $8.5million.

I headed up to Tim's office feeling like frazzled brakes that couldn't stop the wheels of an out-of-control car. Look, I wanted to tell him, the hotel is sold out. The casino is jammed packed. Every restaurant has a wait. We've pulled it off! And tomorrow morning we're going to get the numbers and find out we got killed. What are we doing?

But telling Tim to take back the best gamble in town was like telling Tim not to be *Tim*.

On top of that, if we did take the special odds away from Mr. Royalty, we risked driving him off, never seeing our money again, and having him humiliate us all over town. "Ahhh, The Nugget's too scared to take my bets," would be Mr. Royalty's cherry on top.

Did we want to go through all that? Or did we want to let him back in and pray he didn't swamp us?

Tim was sitting behind his desk in front of an ashtray of dead cigarettes. His tie was loose, and he was staring at the ceiling. A fresh cigarette burned in his hand. Through the smoke curling in the air, I could read a sign on the wall, a sign that he loved, a sign that said: NO ACT OF KINDNESS SHALL GO UNPUNISHED.

Nobody wants to see a friend looking so alone.

Tim got up and grabbed his coat.

"I've gotta go," he said.

. . .

An upper management meeting was scheduled for 10:00 AM the next morning to reevaluate our strategy on extending huge limits. Mr. Royalty was on a run that ultimately beat up not only Las Vegas but casinos as far south as San Diego and as far north as Indiana for more than $25 million. You can talk all the theory and percentages you want. We were losing real money. If Mr. Royalty wasn't stopping at any other casino but The Nugget, *we* could've taken the entire $25 million beating. And who knew when it was going to end.

The meeting was about to start. No Tim.

Calls put through to his office weren't being returned. He wasn't answering his home phone. He wasn't picking up his cell.

I figured he needed time to recover. I figured he'd catch up on the details with Johnny D. over lunch. I knew it was painful for him, much more complex than simply taking an $8 million beating. He knew in his bones he was right. He knew he just had to ride it out. Maybe he wanted to be by himself because riding it out alone made it easier.

I didn't think like a gambler. And he had to be feeling some guilt over how the beating was tearing me apart.

Lunchtime came and went. Johnny D. hadn't seen Tim. The more people couldn't find him, the more they called me.

"Hey, Tom, where's Tim?"

"Where's Tim?"

"Where's Tim?"

"Where's Tim?"

"Where's Tim?"

I couldn't tell if I was frustrated or nervous.

Finally, I took the elevator up to the Steve Wynn Suite where Tim occasionally spent the night. I slipped my master key into the lock, opened the door, and stepped into a haze of smoke. Cans of Red Bull energy drinks were scattered around the room. Ashtrays were full. There was Tim—lying under the covers in bed. He hadn't shaved. His clothes were wrinkled. He looked like he hadn't slept in weeks.

In that moment, all of the money and the limits and the strategy went right out the window.

I pulled a chair up to the edge of the bed. "Are you all right?" I asked.

What followed wasn't exactly a golden moment in our friendship.

But maybe you've got to go through moments like that to make a friendship golden in the first place.

CHAPTER 2

THE WISE GUY

Now, of course, Tim has a very different memory of the afternoon after twenty-two straight.

"What are you, crazy? I was fine."

"Tim, you weren't returning any calls."

"I'd just lost more than $8 million! Who would I want to talk to?"

"Tim, the haze in that room was so thick it was like walking into an opium den."

"So I've been known to smoke a cigarette or two."

"Tim, you were shaking."

"Get out of here! If I lost every cent that I have, I don't think I'd shake."

"Tim—"

"Tom, you are such a square from Barnsville. All we needed was more time."

"Tim, you know th—"

"Look, I'm the gambler here. So now you're makin' me out to be Mary Poppins."

And that's what makes Tim *Tim*.

When you get down to basics, nothing about Tim Poster has changed since the day I met him.

It was the fall of 1989. Nobody had mobile phones back then. Nobody I knew, anyway, and certainly no college students. Maybe executives of huge corporations did. And Tim.

He was a junior at the University of Southern California. And he drove down I-5 from USC to USD—the University of San Diego—to visit a high school buddy.

His buddy, Lorenzo Fertitta, was my college roommate.

It's a running joke that I owe a huge debt of gratitude to the director of housing at USD for assigning me to a room with Lorenzo and setting the wheels of my partnership with Tim in motion. But that's a little off base. Lorenzo and I were assigned to the same dorm. We decided to room with each other off campus in our junior year. One thing's for sure. It's impossible to know where life would have taken me if I'd never met Lorenzo.

The Fertitta family owns Station Casinos in Las Vegas. For me, just meeting somebody with a background like Lorenzo's was an eye-opener. But nothing I'd seen during a few visits to his home could have prepared me for Tim.

Meeting Tim was like stepping into a James Caan movie. Tim held this big, black brick-of-a-phone to his ear as he paced back and forth blurting out the lines of Sunday's football games. I'm not sure if he even noticed me. It was as if his entire existence was hanging in the balance between "Pittsburgh minus 6" and "Denver plus 7."

The instant that really stuck with me, though, came an hour

later when we sat down for lunch at this little Italian restaurant called Sardina's. I was looking at the menu the way a student with $500 spending money for the entire semester looks at a menu. When I saw a sandwich in one column connected to an $8 price tag in the other, I got nervous.

"Hey, let me get this," Tim said.

And I knew. I knew he could tell by the way I was looking at the menu that I didn't have much money. But there was something about his offer that was so genuine it was impossible for me to feel awkward.

It's hard to explain that moment. Sure, the bond I'd developed with Lorenzo over two years made me open to Tim. And how could anyone meeting this guy *not* be curious? But from that moment on, something inside me trusted him.

"You get the next one." Tim said, which is exactly what he said the *next* time a waiter put down the check.

What I didn't realize at the time was that Tim didn't have much money himself. Whatever he had, he carried in his pocket. And whatever was in his pocket, he was going to spend — because he was confident he'd fill up his pocket again.

Booking games came as natural to Tim as making ketchup to a Heinz. My family watched football games on Sunday and rooted for the Vikings. Tim's family reached for the Doritos and screamed for the point spread.

So much of everything that's happened to us can be traced to timing. It goes back years before we met, when a law was passed allowing casinos in Nevada to open sports books. Anybody entering a casino these days sees sports books with cushy seats and drink holders, a feast of giant screens and flashing scoreboards. It's hard to imagine that these parlors didn't exist back in the '60s. In those days, casinos were only able to offer table games and slots.

The law permitting these sports books brought Tim's family from Pittsburgh to Vegas in 1975. His Uncle Jack was one of the best odds makers in town. And he got Tim's dad a job with the sports book at the Stardust. Tim's family had little money. But Uncle Jack was connected.

Those early days gave Tim the impression that anything was possible in Las Vegas. While Tim's mom and dad looked for a place to settle, the family stayed in a room comped by the Sands Hotel. Among Tim's first memories of Vegas is going down to the coffee shop as a six-year-old, meeting Eddie the host, and asking if it were okay to get some breakfast. Eddie would call over to the person in charge, hold up his right arm, and point at Tim. It meant hold the check. The meal was free. That magical sensation never left Tim. When he picked up the phone in his room, asked for pancakes, and twenty minutes later a guy rolled them in on a cart, he felt like the most important first grader in the world.

He saw the name Dean Martin on billboards, heard the name over the television news, and the next thing he knew Deano was lifting him up and putting a $100 bill in his hand.

It took Tim a little while to realize it wasn't *Dean* Martin who'd handed him the C-note, but *Bob* Martin. And a little longer to realize what a legend Bob Martin was in his own right.

Bob was one of the great sports bookies of all time. To this day, Tim can recite the wisdom Bob passed down over the years in a gravel voice that was flavored by nonfiltered Camels and pours of Jack Daniel's. "If you think you've got the best of it," Bob would say, "take dead aim and hold onto your balls."

That's how a man came to wear $900 silk shirts in Las Vegas.

"If you lose, learn to shrug your shoulders and say, 'I'm still gonna have the same breakfast tomorrow.'"

But above all, "Don't ever forget the single most thrilling thing in the world is to gamble and win. And the second most is to gamble and lose."

Uncle Jack's buddies added other gems like "Have a couple of thousand in your pocket at all times. When you get up in the morning to take a piss, bring your bankroll to the bathroom just in case something happens along the way."

Tim inhaled these mottos until they were his own. His entire world was framed by gambling. A great Sunday morning as a boy meant a trip to the buffet at The Golden Nugget with his parents after mass. A sad Friday night meant that a family vacation to Disneyland had been canceled without a word because his dad had lost a big bet. When Tim's dad left home, his Uncle Jack and Uncle Jimmy stepped in to help raise him. They continued his education with stories about the famed restaurateur Joe "The Pig" Pignatello, who learned how to cook from Al Capone's mother and was a personal chef to Sam Giancana and Frank Sinatra. Joe was a degenerate gambler who'd scratch out the prices on the fancy menus at his joint and scribble in higher ones to compensate for unfortunate rolls of the dice.

It was only natural that Tim would become best buddies with a kid named Frank Toti, whose dad, Big Frank, ran the Barbary Coast. Big Frank would take the two boys up on the catwalks above the casino where men with binoculars spied on the blackjack players to see if they were counting cards. This was back in the day before the cameras were honed.

"How do you count cards?" Tim asked.

"It's not that hard," Big Frank said. "I can show you."

"Really?"

It was an education that you couldn't get at Bishop Gorman High School. But the school offered something else that was truly amazing. It's almost impossible to believe the connections available to a kid who simply walked through the doors of Bishop Gorman in 1983.

In a single classroom you could find:

Lorenzo Fertitta, who'd become one of the principal owners of fifteen casinos as the vice-chairman and president of Station Casinos, who would also go on to own the Ultimate Fighting Championship, and whose older brother, Frank, would guide the family empire with him.

Tim Poster, who'd come up with the concept for a travel-booking company that would take off with the Internet and be bought by Expedia for more than $100 million.

And Perry Rogers, whose best friend was Andre Agassi, and who'd come to make multimillion-dollar deals down the road as an agent representing his childhood buddy and basketball star Shaquille O'Neal.

You know how Perry met Tim? He sat behind him as a freshman in social studies class simply because Tim's last name starts with a *p* and Perry's begins with an *r*. Six minutes into the first class, Tim turned to Perry and said, "Hey, buddy, you got 25 bucks?"

"What?" Perry asked.

"Look," Tim said. "The Showboat has this contest. Takes $50 to enter. You pick every NFL game for the whole season. If you have the best record at the end of the year, you win a house. I got $25. But I don't got $50. You got 25 bucks?"

"Yeah," Perry said, "I got 25 bucks."

So they went in together. They got beaten up pretty good that first week, and winning the top prize was out of the question. So Tim said, "I've got an idea: Let's shoot for Fiddle in the Middle!" That was the prize awarded to anyone who could compile a record at the end of the season that was exactly .500.

They didn't win that, either. But the consolation prize was the biggest of all. They got to know each other, and after more than twenty years and some million-dollar deals together, Perry is still shaking his head and smiling at the memory of Fiddle in the Middle.

It wasn't long before everybody at Bishop Gorman knew Tim. Tim and Little Frank became the school bookies. There was nothing at all clandestine about the operation. "Hey, what's the line on Baltimore?" other kids would shout as Tim and Little Frank walked the halls or ate in the cafeteria. There were even teachers who bet with them. If this is hard to fathom, you've got to remember that gambling is legal in Las Vegas. It's in the air. At graduation services in the school chapel, casino chips are welcome in the collection plate.

Sure, you're supposed to be 21 to bet. But Tim couldn't help it if he felt 37 when he was 14. And Little Frank had gotten a pretty good education in public relations at the Barbary Coast. The two were thoughtful enough to pass along a book of comp tickets for the restaurants at the Barbary Coast to the dean of students "just in case it comes in handy."

Occasionally, a kid would lose his lunch money for a week to Tim and Little Frank, and his mother would go into the dean of students to complain. So the dean would call Tim and Little Frank into his office for a chat to keep them in line and get an idea who was betting what. Tim and Little Frank would pass on a tidbit of information, and the conversation would degenerate to laughter. "What?" the dean of students would say. "Curt Magleby bet the *Cubs*?"

Cubs games were one of the most frequently bet because there were no lights at Wrigley Field back then, and the games started in the afternoon. The two-hour time difference allowed Tim to get in the first action of the day at 11:00 AM. It was hot stuff back then to have a sports pager. In those days a pager was the size of a pack of cigarettes, and it cost about $400 a month to access the constant updates. But classes had a little more juice with the beeper announcing every run scored and change of inning.

Apparently, one teacher was not at all amused. Mr. Ward taught business just before lunch—exactly the time the games at Wrigley Field started. "I know you've got one of those damn beeper things," he said as Tim approached the classroom one day. "Do you have it on you now?"

"What are you talking about?" Tim shot back. With all due respect to honesty, no self-respecting bookie was going to surrender his beeper to his fourth-period business teacher.

"*You* know what I'm talking about," Ward said. "If you have it on you now, I want it. You are not to bring it into my classroom! And if you do bring it into my classroom, I'm kicking you out!"

Tim had it safely tucked away in his pants and clicked off. He was home free. "I have no idea what you're talking about," he said.

The class started and as soon as the first pitch was thrown at Wrigley Field, the service confirmed the starting pitchers with a beep, beep, beep.

An "oh, shit" feeling spread through Tim's belly. It *wasn't* clicked off.

"Poster!" Mr. Ward howled. "You're out of here!"

Tim made the long walk to the dean's office.

"Dean, you gotta bail me out here," he said. "Ward wants me out for good. Somehow, you've got to square this up."

The dean of students deftly arranged for Tim's return to class. Perhaps he had a sense of Tim's potential. Though he had no concept of the money being run through Tim and Frank's notebooks during Tim's senior year. If he'd seen what was going on during the run-up to the night Sugar Ray Leonard challenged Marvelous Marvin Hagler for the world middleweight championship at Caesars Palace, the dean would've gasped.

When you talk to people who were in Vegas back in 1987, they remember it as the last great fight of the city's golden age of boxing.

Leonard had won an Olympic gold medal. His blend of dazzling speed, power, matinee idol looks, and charisma had made him the sport's biggest star by the early '80s. And his reputation as one of the greats at 147 pounds was sealed when he came from behind with one eye battered shut to win by technical knockout over Tommy Hearns in the fourteenth round of one of the best fights ever. Shortly afterward, though, he suffered a detached retina and retired.

In the meantime, Marvelous Marvin Hagler stormed through the middleweight division. He was bald-headed, ripped, and fierce—a relentless warrior. He hadn't lost a fight in eleven years and seemed to be at the height of his powers when Leonard decided to come out of retirement to challenge him at 160 pounds.

To Tim and Frank, this was a no-brainer. Leonard didn't have a chance. He hadn't fought in three years and was sure to be rusty. Plus, he was moving up in weight to fight a naturally bigger and stronger man. What's more, Hagler was a beast in the gym and definitely figured to be sky high for the fight.

The outcome seemed so clear to Tim and Little Frank that they overlooked the fundamental rule of bookmaking. In a perfect world, the bookmaker balances bets on both sides and makes his money from a percentage of all the action.

Tim and Frank were so sure that Hagler was going to win they refused to take any bets on him. If you wanted to bet the fight with Tim and Frank, you had to put your money on Leonard.

That gives you a little insight on Tim. *If you think you've got the best of it, take dead aim and hold onto your balls.* But it also gives you a little insight on Lorenzo.

Lorenzo never made a bet with Tim and Frank. Never. But his ears perked up as he sat in English class listening to Tim rant on and on about how Leonard was going to be demolished.

Lorenzo had been to a lot of the big fights. He loved Leonard's style and thought his speed and footwork would confuse and fluster Hagler.

"Okay," Lorenzo said. "I'll bet $100 on Leonard."

It was the equivalent of a high school kid putting up a thousand bucks today.

"I'll give you 7-1," Tim shot back.

"I want a parlay," Lorenzo said. "I also want Leonard by decision."

"A parlay on Leonard! You've got to be kidding me! I'll give you 11-1!"

The fight took place on a Monday night. Payoff days at Bishop Gorman were always Fridays. If you'd done business with Tim and Little Frank in the past and were deemed a valued customer, you didn't have to put up any money in advance. But if you hadn't bet with them and they didn't know your credit history, then you might be asked to put up the cash in advance.

There was a lot of new action on Leonard, and so Tim and

Little Frank took in a lot of cash before the fight. They then turned around and used *that* money to bet on Hagler—along with just about every other dime they owned.

The evening was electric, and Tim and Little Frank had seats somewhere in the rafters. From way up in row ZZ, though, it was hard to see exactly what was going on. Leonard had turned back the clock. For the first four rounds he flashed around the ring as if he were in his prime, darting in to land combinations and escaping pretty much unscathed.

Maybe Lorenzo understood that Hagler was the type of fighter who always won the rematches big—but who had trouble figuring out his opponents the first time around. Anyway, it was pretty clear by the start of the fifth round that there were only two ways for Hagler to win. He had to take seven of the next eight rounds on the judges' scorecards or score a knockout.

Hagler began to impose his will in round five. Tim's hopes swelled in six, seven, and eight. Then came the ninth round—a classic—with the two fighters trading toe-to-toe. Hagler was landing with authority, but Leonard's flurries were like fireworks that lifted the crowd to its feet. As the bell sounded to end the round, an "oh, shit" feeling began to spread through Tim's belly.

Hagler pushed forward in the final rounds and drew closer and closer. Leonard seemed exhausted and out of answers as the clock wound down. It was tight. Nobody could know how the judges would score it. But everyone knew what the outcome would have been if the fight had gone one more round. If Hagler had just had a little more time . . .

The decision and the championship went to Leonard.

Tim and Frank were high school kids who'd lost every penny they owned and were now twenty grand in the hole.

Nobody at school thought they'd show up the next day and

certainly not on Friday. But there wasn't much compassion. The code was clear. Anyone who won a bet from Tim and Little Frank knew they would be paid in full, just as they knew they had to pay off their own losses. There was a rumor that the biggest kid in the class, Bert, made visits to anyone who didn't pay off their debts to Tim and Little Frank. The story was that Bert had been brought into the operation as muscle, and that he'd get half of what he could shake out of any debtors. It was pure bullshit, but Tim and Little Frank never denied it because it made the collection process go much smoother.

The stakes were high. If Tim and Frank couldn't pay off their bets, no matter what happened down the road, that's the way they'd be marked for the rest of their lives. They'd have broken the code. In a town that from its inception grew up outside the law, all a man has is his word.

As soon as the decision was announced, both Tim and Little Frank (now a prominent lawyer, by the way) realized there was only one way to get that kind of money, and they headed straight for the Barbary Coast.

There was a big postfight party at the hotel. The Barbary Coast had taken a beating on the fight, too. But a party is a party. Little Frank and Tim waited around all night trying to get up the nerve to bring up their predicament to Big Frank. At four o'clock in the morning, they sat down in the coffee shop for some Chinese food and explained the situation.

Big Frank understood, and he backed them. It's moments like those that explain why Tim Poster is the most loyal friend a guy could ever find.

He showed up at school a few hours later in the same clothes without a wink of sleep.

It certainly would have been understandable if Tim had

prefaced his payoffs that Friday with "you lucky son-of-a-bitch." The fight was razor close and the decision controversial. But that's not how he settled up.

"Everybody loves a winner," he sang with a smile as he counted out the cash. "Remember, baseball season is right around the corner."

By the end of baseball season, Tim and Little Frank had paid Big Frank back every cent.

There are tons of stories from Tim's childhood. I could go on all day. But that might give you the impression that Tim was a stereotypical bookie. And that would paint a shallow picture of an American original. Yeah, you could see him as a baby Joe Pesci in a mob movie. But he was also like the mathematician in A Beautiful Mind who could grasp a blackboard full of numbers in an instant. Plus, he had an amazing work ethic.

There's an old expression that goes "Personality is what you see and character is what you are." It's easy to see the guy with the sports beeper and the cash. But not many people get close enough to see all the qualities inside Tim. Only a few have gotten a true glimpse of his mind or his work ethic. Didn't matter whether he was valet parking or answering the phones at a room reservation service while he was in high school. Any coworker who wanted a day off to take out his girlfriend or a night off to check out the lap dancers knew he could always call Tim to fill in.

Tim's job booking hotel room reservations over the phone was the seed that led to our travel business. It didn't take a mind like Tim's very long to compute just how lucrative the reservation business could be. He'd take a call for a weekend room reservation. The rate at the Sahara was, say, $50 a night. That put the cost for the two nights at $100. Tim then called the Sahara and booked the room. After the room was used and paid for, the Sahara sent 10 or 15 percent—a check for $10 or $15—back to the company that employed Tim.

The reservations were all recorded on sheets. On the nights that Tim closed the office, it was his job to total the numbers. "Man," he'd tell himself. "That's a lot of money for just answering the phone."

Later, at USC, Tim took an entrepreneurial class in which he was asked to invent a business and then devise a plan to show how it could prosper. It was the work of an entire semester. Tim came up with a model for a hotel booking business that had the potential to be much more profitable than the one he already knew was lucrative.

In Tim's model, the merchant model, he'd go directly to the Sahara and ask for a block of rooms at a wholesale rate. He'd get that same $50 room at the Sahara, say, for $40. Then, when a person called up for a weekend reservation, Tim would charge the guy's credit card $100 for the same two nights. So Tim's profit was roughly $20 for the same transaction.

There were additional benefits to the merchant model. Tim would be charging the customer making the reservation by credit card on the day of the call—even if the person didn't use the room until three months down the road. So Tim was holding the money for those three months before he got a bill from the Sahara, a bill that he might not pay until a few weeks after it arrived.

The genius behind this model is that everybody wins. The Sahara's happy because it's filling up rooms without having to spend more on marketing. The customer has the convenience of one-stop shopping at prices lower than he'd get directly from the hotel. And Tim's model not only generated a better profit, but it also generated interest on the money he was holding.

As his junior year wound down, Tim figured he could actually pull his plan off. But he'd already lined up a summer job in finance with the L.A. office of a Wall Street firm called Kidder Peabody. In a strange way, this is where luck came in.

Tim started the summer job running errands for an executive, but showed up one morning to find the executive's office completely empty. The executive had vanished in the middle of the night. Tim blinked and wondered if he was in the right place.

When he asked what was going on, he realized that nobody knew who he was. He'd just started. Nobody else in the office had really noticed him. Finally, he found out that the executive had left for another firm. Before leaving in darkness, the exec had passed on a good word about Tim to the managing director.

The managing director called Tim in for a meeting and told him to leave his phone number, that the firm would call him as soon as a similar opening developed.

Tim had to make a decision. Stay in L.A. and wait? Or go back to Vegas? He still had three semesters to go before he graduated. He had virtually no money outside of what was in his pocket. No checking account. No office. And if he started a company, he'd only have three months to get the business up and running before heading back to school.

He zipped out letters to the sales departments of thirty hotels in Las Vegas, explaining the creation of his business and asking them if he could get blocks of rooms at wholesale rates. Then he stood with this batch of letters outside a mailbox on Jefferson and Figueroa at the entrance to USC without the slightest clue what would happen if he dropped them in.

When you've got nothing, he reminded himself, you've got nothing to lose. He tossed the envelopes in the slot.

He returned to Vegas and finagled an office that was big enough for a desk, a phone, a chair, and a pillow. He set up an 800 number. Then one day he found a contract in the mail from a hotel called the San Remo (now Hooters) that offered him a block of rooms and asked for a $500 deposit. He walked over and paid in cash. His friendship with Lorenzo got him some rooms at the Palace Station owned by the Fertittas with nothing down.

Once again, his timing couldn't have been more perfect. He opened his business during the summer of 1990. Only half a year earlier, in November of 1989, a man-made volcano erupted over The Strip in front of a hotel called the Mirage. Steam, water, and flames blasted 40 feet in the air to the amazement of thousands of onlookers. The Mirage was the brainchild of Steve Wynn. Las Vegas had never seen anything like it, and the tourism industry erupted, as well.

"Looking back," Tim would say, "starting the reservation business at that time was like being the guy who paid $24 to the Indians for Manhattan."

All Tim needed to do to catch the overflow of demand was to make his company known—and he knew just how to do it. While at USC, he often read the Calendar section in the Sunday *Los Angeles Times*. It mostly covered the local arts scene, concerts, movies, and shows, but it also contained a section about Las Vegas. Every hotel in Vegas advertised in it.

Tim sketched out an ad that read:

LAS VEGAS HOTEL RESERVATIONS
LOWEST RATES
ONE CALL DOES IT ALL

Then he amplified his 800 number as large as could be fit in a tiny two-inch by four-inch box.

He only had rooms at two hotels to offer, but he knew he'd figure out a way to work around his limitations once the phone started ringing. His real problem was that he'd exhausted his bankroll on the office, and the account exec for the *Los Angeles Times* who'd stopped by to meet him wanted $3,250 for the ad contract up front.

"I don't have my checks with me," Tim told the guy. "I'll have to FedEx you one."

The guy told Tim the check had to get to the *Times* by Thursday in order for the ad to appear in the Sunday paper.

Tim took dead aim and held onto his balls.

He figured if he FedExed a check on Wednesday for afternoon delivery, it would arrive in Los Angeles just on time—late Thursday.

But it would be too late for the newspaper to get the check to the bank before it closed that day. Which meant it would get to the newspaper's bank on Friday, and arrive at Tim's bank on Monday at the earliest. Basically, Tim would have to generate $3,250 in revenue on Sunday, his first day of business, to cover the check. If his first check to the *L.A. Times* bounced, well, as Tim would say, finito.

When Tim walked into his office early Sunday morning, the phone was ringing. Not only that, but his Radio Shack answering system had a ton of messages on it. Tim tried to keep up with the demand all day. If people requested any hotel other than the Sam Remo or Palace Station, he told them that unfortunately it was sold out on that date. Or else he quoted a ridiculously high price that he knew the customers wouldn't go for—which allowed him to steer them toward the San Remo or Palace Station. If people insisted on staying at the Flamingo, he booked the reservation himself for the 10 percent travel agent fee. He cleared out his answering machine and took calls until almost 10:00 PM.

By 6:00 AM Monday morning, the company handling the credit card transactions had deposited Tim's first day of revenue in his checking account. There would be no sweating that check. Las Vegas Reservation Systems was in business.

When Tim got to the office an hour later, the mailbox on his answering machine was maxed out.

CHAPTER 3

THE SQUARE

Just as there was a moment for me, there was a moment for Tim.

While Tim doesn't recall offering to buy me that sandwich at Sardina's, he does remember the first moment he trusted me. And, of course, it's a moment that completely passed *me* by.

One day, after graduating from college, I showed up at his LVRS office to meet him. An unattended phone rang and I picked it up, grabbed a pen, took the message, and passed the information on to him. It was the most natural thing in the world. So there's no way a moment like that would stand out in my mind. But it stayed with Tim.

It astonishes me when I look back on it. Hundreds of millions of dollars would be made from a partnership based on trust, and that trust was rooted in the ordering of a sandwich and the answering of a phone.

I hadn't given the slightest thought to working with Tim when I graduated from college. My goal was to be the next Bob Costas.

I got my first television job in a small town in the desert between San Diego and Las Vegas. If you've never heard of Victorville, California, maybe you've heard of Roy Rogers and Dale Evans. That was their home. Victorville's top attraction back then was a statue of Roy's horse, Trigger, rearing up on its hind legs in the center of town. You get the picture.

The sports job at KHIZ was already taken. I started as the weatherman. Sometimes I phoned Tim before I went on the air to ask him the temperature in Las Vegas. "It's hot," he'd say.

On the surface, being a weatherman in the desert may not seem like the most challenging of jobs. But I learned how to react when the 112-degree temperatures knocked out the power and the teleprompter failed in the middle of a segment. I learned how to make a feature on the prizewinning goat at the county fair grab your attention. It wasn't long before I was covering the Lady Jackrabbits basketball team at Victor Valley High School and sitting in the sports anchor seat. You know what? It was *great.* I had the opportunity to soak in every detail about communicating through television and took advantage of every minute. I learned how to speak with proper diction, how to feel at ease in front of a camera, and how to edit my own pieces.

But a year later, I was still 2,800 miles from ESPN headquarters in Bristol, Connecticut. And I was making $12,000 a year. It was hard to imagine Bob Costas living on ramen noodles in an apartment with a fake fireplace.

The lights of Las Vegas were less than three hours away, and I took off to see Tim and Lorenzo whenever I could. Tim could make an ordinary day extraordinary. A trip to Vegas might mean a seat at an Evander Holyfield fight through one of Uncle Jack's connections. Or dinner on the town with Uncle Jimmy. Meals were not meals for Uncle Jimmy. They were events.

When Uncle Jimmy entered a room, it sparkled like a pinky ring. Fancy suits. Dark glasses. Being around Uncle Jimmy was like stepping into a Scorsese film. Seating me at Uncle Jimmy's table must've been as comical as dropping Uncle Jimmy into Disney World. And I know exactly how that would play out because it actually happened, and Tim's friend Cedric loves to tell the story.

At lunchtime, Tim, Cedric, and Uncle Jimmy were strolling through the world food court at Epcot Center, past restaurants offering dozens of cuisines, when they decided to go Italian. They entered what was by no means a fine restaurant. It was sort of like a giant cafeteria with teenagers making pasta in the window. Uncle Jimmy looked at the menu and asked the waiter about the veal piccata.

The waiter told him that it was great.

Uncle Jimmy slowly swiveled his head to reconfirm the setting and expressed his suspicions.

The waiter assured him the veal piccata would be to his liking.

Uncle Jimmy warned the waiter that if it wasn't done right, he was going to send it back.

A few minutes later, the waiter returned with fettucini for Tim and Cedric, and he set down the veal piccata in front of Uncle Jimmy.

Uncle Jimmy started working the plate over with knife and fork, maneuvering the food around, because it had to be set just right before it was worthy of a bite. Finally, he carefully sliced a piece of veal, took a bite, and looked up, "Where is that guy?"

The waiter came over, and Uncle Jimmy said, "You call this veal piccata?"

The next thing you know the head chef was wheeling the entire spice rack on a cart out to Uncle Jimmy. And Uncle Jimmy was pulling off the oregano, the salt, the garlic, and the basil and showing the chef the proper way to prepare the dish. When he was finished, he took a bite, turned to the chef and said, "Now, *that's* veal piccata."

And *that* was normal to Tim, his family, and his friends.

I was the oddity. The Square John from Barnsville. You could imagine Uncle Jimmy's eyes widening when I mentioned that the best steak I'd ever tasted was on a Northwest Airlines flight. Or Tim slapping his forehead when my younger brother, John, once referred to the favorite in a football game as "the overdog."

But there was something endearing about it to them, and they embraced me as family. I know I felt like part of the clan, because I remember being hit hard by Uncle Jimmy's death. When I came up to Las Vegas to celebrate Christmas in 1992, Tim was still hurting. Maybe he wanted to get as far as he possibly could from the pain of a Christmas without Uncle Jimmy. Out of nowhere, he said, "I want to see where you're from."

"Sure," I said.

"Let's go right now."

So we went to the airport and got on an empty flight leaving the evening of Christmas. We landed in Minneapolis at 7:00 AM. The temperature was five below zero. Tim rented a Cadillac, and we headed down the frosted highway to my hometown.

To most people, Burnsville, Minnesota, would not exactly qualify for the nickname "Barnsville." It's a quiet, middle-class suburb south of Minneapolis consisting of nicely landscaped homes. But as Tim veered through the streets of my neighborhood and passed yard after yard decked out with giant plastic

Santa Clauses along with blinking lights and electronically trotting reindeer , he could only shake his head and whisper, "This is not the real world."

We passed all the lawns I'd mowed in the summer and all the driveways I'd shoveled in winter. We passed all the front doors I'd determinedly walked the *Minneapolis Star and Tribune* up to on my paper route instead of hurling the newspaper on the grass. We passed the two houses I'd grown up in—basketball court in the driveway, swimming pool in the backyard.

Nearly anyone else in America listening to the description of my childhood—the red Schwinn bicycle with the banana seat, the Little League baseball, basketball, and soccer games, the skiing, cookouts, and zooms down Bob Lurtsema's water slide—would've seen me as the typical suburban kid who grew up next door. In Tim's eyes, I was unique.

If it wasn't for Tim, I might never have understood how not so typical I am. We all have different fingerprints. But we rarely put a magnifying glass to them. Sometimes we don't realize everything that we have inside of us. When I do look closely, I can only shake my head. The odds that my mom and dad—a farm girl from Minnesota and an Air Force pilot from Chicago—would meet at a certain moment in 1963 in Waikiki had to be more than a million to one.

My dad had finished eighth in a group of about thirty-five pilots in flight school, and the selection process sent him to Hickam Air Force Base in Honolulu. If he had finished seventh, he would've been stationed in California, his life would have been completely different, and I wouldn't be here to tell this story. But he *was* eighth. And that gave him a chance to meet my mom, a nurse who'd heard a doctor in Minneapolis rave about the exotic beaches in Hawaii. On a whim with five other nurses, she lined up a job in Honolulu and rented a house on a hillside behind Diamond Head Volcano. I came into the world because two people with a sense of adventure were in the right place at just the right time. If there's a gene for that, I definitely got it.

The stories I told Tim as we drove through the snow were random. But in them I could hear the influence my parents had had on me. My dad's job as a pilot for Northwest Airlines was an execution of levelheadedness and smooth landings. And my mom could start up a conversation with anyone, which is probably what made an elevator ride with me so astounding to Tim. "If someone gets in an elevator at a hotel with Tom for a five-floor ride," Tim loved to say, "the moment that elevator door opens, Tom will know where they're from and if they're married or single. If it's a ten-floor ride, he'll know how long they're staying and what restaurant they ate at the night before. If it's a twenty-floor ride, he'll know where they're from, how long they'd lived there, what they ate the night before, when their anniversary is, how many kids they've got, and what the kids' names are."

Maybe, as we drove along that day, Tim was making these sorts of connections in his head and wondering how they might relate to his business. He's a great judge of character, and I must've been confirming his instincts as I described what it was like to grow up in the middle of a family with five kids.

My two older brothers used me to practice the moves they saw Andre the Giant execute on professional wrestling—turning me upside down, holding me by the torso, and crashing my head to the floor in the classic Piledriver. But that's what big brothers are for, right? My younger brother came along six years after me on the exact day I was born—so I had to share a birthday with him. I had to give up my room when I was nine on the day my adopted sister came up from Columbia. One thing I learned from my birth order was how to understand everybody's situations and eccentricities. The way to be happy, I've found, is to make sure everyone around you is happy.

Our tour of "Barnsville" headed up the road past Holy Angels High School where my older brothers, Fred and Mike, grew to be six-foot-four varsity basketball stars. As we passed the gym, I told Tim about one of my deepest childhood wounds. It must've seemed trivial as we drove along, and it certainly is now as I look back upon it. But when you're young and vulnerable, a wound can stay with you and influence the rest of your life. You always hear stories like the one about a twelve-year-old kid named Cassius Clay who had his bicycle stolen and went into a boxing gym to learn how to fight so he could beat up the kid who'd taken it. It was the hurt from that stolen bicycle that set him on the road to become Muhammad Ali, heavyweight champion of the world. Look deep enough and you'll see that many of us are formed by our vulnerable moments.

It's hard to be five-feet-nine-inches tall after your two older brothers were six-foot-four high school basketball stars. I worked for years to star on that same high school team and kept waiting to grow into the role. My brothers had measured themselves with pencil lines on the wall of our laundry room, and I just couldn't understand why the top of my head stopped seven inches short of their top marks. I once read that Michael Jordan got cut from his high school team when he was a sophomore, that he knew he had to grow, and that he spent a lot of time over the following summer hanging from monkey bars at a playground as if to will himself into growing taller. And he shot up four inches! Maybe I should have hung from monkey bars.

Instead I compensated for my lack of height in other ways. I didn't try to be like Mike. (Well, sometimes I did—but only on an eight-foot rim.) My heroes were two guys you probably never heard of unless you really follow college basketball: Johnny Dawkins and Tommy Amaker.

They played for Duke, and they were as close as two fingers on the same hand. In fact, their coach, Mike Krzyzewski, taught his players to come together like five fingers into a fist. I spent hours watching Amaker, the playmaker, and Dawkins, the shooter, on television with my backcourt partner, Chris Bednarz. Then the two of us would go out and practice until neither one of us even had to look to know where our other half was. We just knew.

It was obvious that I was never going to be the star of the team. But I thought if I could understand the eccentricities of my teammates and make everyone around me better, then I could get into the starting lineup. I sensed it was all about the extras. So when the coach asked for laps, I ran extras. When he asked for free throws, I shot extras. Maybe my Charlie Hustle attitude came simply from being five-foot-nine in a family of six-foot-four-inch high school basketball stars. When the waiters at the deli where I worked over the summer didn't want to make chocolate sundaes because the ice cream in the bin was rock hard and a pain in the ass to scoop out, they always turned to Tommy the busboy. In my own way, I willed myself into becoming the best point guard at Holy Angels High School.

Then the coach told me I wasn't going to start. The younger player coming along behind me was taller and more talented. I couldn't argue the fact that he had more potential. But he didn't have my experience, and he couldn't synthesize like I could. No two ways about it. I was the best guy at my position.

Maybe it was the way the coach told me. All I heard in his tone was: It doesn't matter how hard you try or how successful you are on this court. *You're not playing*.

I hated those words. To this day, I hate those words.

It was hard enough to walk in the laundry room and see the pencil marks on the wall. Hard enough being the kid who got Bs in math after studying longer and harder than his older brothers who'd brought home As. But the coach's rejection cut deeper than not fitting into the family footsteps. It wasn't fair and I felt betrayed. I remember wanting to hit the coach. Of course, I wasn't going to hit him. But I *felt* like it. And I never get into fights.

Well, I did get to start once. Several of our players got suspended for drinking, and one of them was the player at the starting position. The coach had no choice but to start me even though we were playing against the best team in the league. Our opponent, Totino-Grace, was not only undefeated, the game took place on their home court. It was David against Goliath, and the stakes were high. We needed to win to make the playoffs.

Now, I'm not going to compare the game to the movie *Rudy*. But every player on my team came by in the locker room beforehand to let me know that he'd be putting out as much as I would now that I was finally getting my shot.

Chris Bednarz and I went nuts. We dove for and got to every loose ball. I don't think I missed a shot. We won, and our whole team came off the court hollering, high-fiving, and hugging.

You can really get to know someone when you travel with them. Tim just drove and listened.

Everything must've clicked to Tim. A guy who saw his childhood vacation to Disneyland canceled without a word the night before if his dad lost a big bet intuited the symmetry in a partner who grew up knowing exactly when and where his family vacation was going to be: the first week of every August at our family reunion in Grand Rapids, Minnesota. For heaven's sake, I could even tell you what we'd be eating nine months in advance: steaks and walleye, vegetable stir-fry, with blueberry buckle for dessert.

I had no idea what was on Tim's mind as we continued our tour through Barnsville. If you had asked me to name a successful partnership back then, I might have answered Fred Flintstone and Barney Rubble. Most people don't stop and analyze what goes into making a great partnership—even though we find ourselves partnered up by life all the time. It wasn't until years later, after I met Tony and Danny Bennett, that I really began to understand the chemistry behind how Tim and I functioned.

But Tim sensed the magic from the outset. There were times when he was alone in his office, when numbers were speeding his mind off to some uncharted place, and he didn't want to be disturbed by anybody. Call him up at that moment and he was liable to answer the phone, say, "Not now!" and hang up. He didn't like to have to sit down with an employee who wasn't up to snuff and have to fire him. What better characteristic could he look for in a partner than someone who could communicate and make everybody in the company feel at ease?

Not only were Tim's weaknesses my strengths, but we shared strengths. Tim's company was in the travel industry, and he knew that I'd loved to travel since the days I'd put on a jacket and tie and head off to Scotland when a seat was available on a Northwest Airline flight my dad was piloting. Plus, our passion for sports had given us both a fascination for new technology. Tim used the sports pager and brick cell phone well ahead of their time to get gambling information. And long before there was an Internet, my college internship at Channel 10 in San Diego had forced me to grab information off the wire services on the computer. Even though we didn't know it, sports had set our feet in the future.

By late afternoon, we'd wound our way alongside Lake Calhoun, which was frozen in the dead of winter.

"You know, I've never walked on a lake," Tim said. He stopped the car, got out with the engine running, and shut the door.

"Aren't you going to turn the car off?" I asked.

He held up another pair of keys and locked the door. "I asked for an extra pair at the rental counter," he said. "You mean in all your years of living in Minnesota, you never left the car running to keep it warm?"

Never in twenty-two years. But then, when it hit thirty degrees in winter, we were out playing in short pants.

Tim shook his head, rolled his eyes, and headed out to the lake. At first he stepped gingerly, suspiciously chipping his feet at the snow to check the ice underneath. Once he was certain it would support him, he took a few steps and relaxed. Then he started running a few strides and sliding. Soon, he was as giddy as a first grader in a baseball cap with missing front teeth.

I packed a snowball and got ready to throw it, you know, to give him a taste of ice running down the back of his neck. But he turned just in time.

"Don't you fuckin' dare!" he said, pointing a finger like he was Joe Pesci or something.

I laughed, and we walked out even further, hands in our pockets, hearing our feet crunch toward the middle of this empty white sheet.

"You know," Tim broke the silence. "You should come work with me."

He'd hinted at this before, but always in a joking way. This time, he was dead serious.

"You're great with people. I'm great with numbers. You love to travel. This is all about travel. It's in your blood. It's in my blood. We'd be partners: fifty-fifty."

He knew he was asking me to give up my dream. But he also knew that I was beginning to see how difficult it would be to work my way across the country to ESPN. I'd been shocked to discover that broadcasters were changing their names to appear Hispanic in order to get a leg up in certain markets. As much as I liked tamales, I couldn't imagine my German grandfather and Norwegian grandmother flicking the TV on in the living room of their corn farm and hearing me introduce myself as Tomo Banderas.

"Look, if you come into the business with me," Tim said, "you don't have to depend on other people to advance. You don't have to rely on other people to create your opportunities. We control our own destiny."

He was right. My future was in the hands of some TV station owner or producer I hadn't yet met.

"Trust me, Tom, this is a great business, and it's growing like crazy."

Tim went into the full sales pitch. He'd doubled his company's revenue from $800,000 in the first year to $1.6 million in the second. The Vegas boom was just beginning, and the business was growing so fast that it was overwhelming. He couldn't do it by himself. He needed somebody who'd work as hard as he did, somebody he could trust.

"You'll be around friends," he said. "You won't be picking up and leaving every year or two and starting all over to advance your career. You'll have a foundation, and we'll be building something huge. We'll each get $25,000 in salaries, and that's just to start."

Twenty-five thousand was twice what I was earning—and I'd have equity in a company. Endless possibilities were rubbing against the end of a dream. It was confusing and overwhelming, but I felt a tingle inside. It *was* an incredible opportunity.

"You know, Tom, when I was in college I read that of all the people who created great fortunes, none of them got it by working for somebody else. Nobody makes it to the Forbes 400 punching the time clock."

What could I say? There was really nothing to argue. I told Tim I needed some time to think about it. Really, I wanted to talk it over with my dad. The first time my father met Tim, he'd reacted with clear-eyed Midwestern skepticism though he didn't express it directly. "Las Vegas," he said instead, "that's not the real world." But I sensed that I already knew my answer.

"Thanks," I told Tim, and we shook hands.

There was a silent moment, and then Tim howled, "It's freezing! Let's get out of here!"

When we got back to the car, the heater was pumping and it was nice and warm in the Caddy. This was a guy who was thinking ahead.

CHAPTER 4

IN-CREDIBLE!

A few weeks later, I got in my Honda Accord with a hundred dollars in my wallet and headed to Vegas.

There was no corner office waiting for me when I walked in for my first day of work at Las Vegas Reservation Systems on January 25, 1993—just a conference table next to Tim's desk. It didn't take long to figure out that the setup was a lot of the reason behind our success.

Our company was like a little boat on the ocean—we felt every wave around us. If a massive operation like American Express had come up with the same idea as Tim and executed it properly, it would have owned the world. But American Express was built like an ocean liner, heavily structured, and the executives at the wheel were way above the swirling foam. They didn't seem to see the sea change occurring in travel booking—until we grew into a big boat and they wanted to buy us.

The more I began to understand what we were doing at LVRS, the more I realized there were a lot of smart people who didn't get it. "Explain this to me again," asked J. A. Tiberti, the owner of a construction company that had built a good chunk of Las Vegas over half a century. "Your company doesn't have anything. But it sells things?"

He was right. Our inventory was virtual: blocks of rooms that didn't physically exist. We didn't have to pay ahead to get the rooms. We didn't have to load them up and take them to a warehouse. We didn't have to maintain an inventory.

All we had to do was sell the rooms and find ways to get more of them. That came as naturally to me as starting a conversation to pick up a new customer on my paper route. Only in Vegas, the ante was raised.

After awhile, I was walking into the Excalibur, where we'd been allotted five rooms per night, and asking for fifty. The hotel fit our market perfectly. It was new, with a medieval ambiance that appealed to families with kids. And it offered inexpensive food and entertainment. The trouble was, the hotel had been consistently selling out on its own. Why in the world would management hand its rooms over to us at a discount?

But nearly twelve thousand additional rooms came into the market when the Luxor, Treasure Island, and MGM Grand were finished. Excalibur was now competing against those twelve thousand rooms, and it was beginning to feel the squeeze.

We were right on top of it. Our proposal to take fifty rooms was timed perfectly, and they came back with an offer to give us twenty-five if we prepaid for them. We didn't have that kind of money to put up. But we had the friendships sealed at Bishop Gorman High School.

"I gotta go see Lorenzo," Tim said.

The guy whom he'd once given an 11-1 parlay on Sugar Ray

Leonard returned the favor by loaning us $300,000 to prepay for the rooms.

We immediately started to sell twenty-five rooms a night, and soon the Excalibur offered us fifty. Once the other hotels saw us selling those fifty, they knew they could trust us with larger blocks.

There's an old saying, "The harder you work, the luckier you get."

Tim began to save great cigars in the humidor to celebrate when we reached milestones like grossing $10,000 a day. We constantly seemed to be moving to new offices at three in the morning (the downtime for calls) to keep up with the demand for more desks, more phones, more operators, and more parking spaces. American Express had those same brick-and-mortar offices stationed all over the world. We were like a kid who kept outgrowing his shoes. Our company would move to bigger offices ten times in eleven years.

When hotels started to give us large blocks of rooms, they began to feel linked to us, and their feedback guided our expansion. The hotels wanted us to fly people in. They wanted us to create air-hotel-car rental packages. They wanted more than a one-time guest. They wanted us to capture markets from all over America, just as the Las Vegas Convention and Visitors Authority was targeting markets for huge trade shows.

We weren't going to set up charter flights. And the largest carrier into Las Vegas, Southwest Airlines, worked exclusively with a competitor and was off limits. So we set our sights on a few others.

And now you'll see why it was so fun to come to work every day. You couldn't create a reality TV show better than what we had going on in our office. It was an amusement park of energy. Even people who weren't working for us—guys like Bob Nagy,

"Naaygs" to us —wanted to come by and dive headfirst down the waterslide.

No scriptwriter could possibly invent Bob Nagy. Naaygs made even the most ordinary backyard picnic introduction unforgettable. We were at the home of our friend Tito Tiberti when Naaygs was presented to us along with two sentences. "I apologize in advance for introducing Bob to you," Tito said. "I take no responsibility for what happens to you next."

How could I possibly describe Naaygs? You can start by trying to imagine a cross between Don King, Archie Bunker, and Louis Rukeyser running a midsized investment firm. A *cheap* cross between Don King, Archie Bunker, and Louis Rukeyser. Tighter than two coats of paint, Tim used to say, shaking his head. The fact that Naaygs was a multimillionaire only made his antics all the more exasperating and comical.

But Naaygs was very successful and capable of lightning-bolt ideas. He was one of those guys who read everything, and for the first five minutes of a conversation could appear to be an expert on whatever subject was tossed his way. He was so persuasive he could convince you to turn off on a highway exit even when you knew it wouldn't take you to the place that you wanted to go. Naaygs pleaded to be part of our presentation to bring the airlines into our fold. It was sheer passion. He wasn't making a cent.

Okay, okay, we said, not exactly sure how he was going to blend with his partner on the assignment. Now, imagine Naaygs paired with our vice president of sales—Richie Rich.

That was our nickname for Michael Reichartz, whose dad had been president of Caesars Palace and who'd grown up playing soccer in the halls of the Waldorf-Astoria.

Richie Rich showed up immaculately dressed for the first airline presentation. Naaygs arrived in our office with the remnants of an omelet on the lapel of his suit—a suit, by the way, which had gone out of style twenty years before. The hem on his pants was coming loose. And his cream-colored socks clashed horribly with the dark hue of his suit. Tim went berserk, half-appalled and half loving it.

"Look at yourself!" he howled. "You got egg on your suit! Your pants are coming undone! Your lapels are too wide! Your tie is too big! Naaygs, what the fuck?"

So Naaygs washed off the eggs, grabbed a stapler, stapled the cuff on his pants leg, turned to Tim, and fired back, "Well, *now* what've you got to say?"

No, this just wasn't going to happen at American Express. And it was only the beginning.

We got Naaygs a new tie and some dark socks and sent him off with Richie Rich to meet an executive from TWA. The meeting was three weeks after the tragic midair explosion of a TWA jet leaving JFK for Paris, and on the drive over Richie Rich cautioned Naaygs about bringing up the incident. Remember, he said, this is simply about putting together vacation packages with Las Vegas Reservation Systems.

As soon as they sat down with the TWA executive, Naaygs opened the conversation with "So what do you think it was?"

"What do I think *what* was?" the TWA exec asked.

"The explosion that took down Flight 800. I think it was a missile. I don't see any other explanation."

Richie Rich ground his teeth and bit his lip all through the meeting, and he really let Naaygs have it on the ride back to the office. By the time we'd all gotten through with him, Naaygs looked like a slapped puppy. He begged us to let him make up for his blunder the following day in the meeting scheduled with United Airlines.

Looking back on it, I can't believe we let him go. But Tim

and I loved him so much we relented. He really was a smart guy. His heart was in the right place. Remember, the guy wasn't getting paid a cent!

The next day, Naaygs and Richie Rich showed up for the meeting with United. The airline's sales manager was an elegant woman named Julia Wong. Very classy. Naaygs was on his best behavior at the start, but as the meeting loosened up he told a story that led to the line, "Yeah, and this guy didn't have a Chinaman's chance of getting promoted. "

Ms. Wong let the comment pass, but when she excused herself a few moments later, Richie Rich stood up and started pummeling Naaygs.

"How could you do this to me two days in a row?" he screamed through clenched teeth.

"What I do?" Naaygs wanted to know.

Well, we ended up getting the account and developing a great relationship with United. (TWA went out of business.) And there was no way Tim would ever keep Naaygs from coming back through our doors because he loved to tell stories about Naaygs as much as he did smoking those landmark cigars.

We were lighting up quite a bit. Our sales numbers were heading through the roof:

1991: $1,600,000
1992: $2,800,000
1993: $3,600,000
1994: $4,800,000
1995: $6,200,000
1996: $8,500,000

No matter how much we grew or where we moved, though, the frat-house element remained in the air. Tim's Aunt Mary, his first unpaid employee, wandered around and scolded whomever she heard cursing "Watch your mouth, boys! This is not a bar and grill. This is a fancy business. You don't use words like that in a classy place." Our rottweiler, Bally, roamed the hallways. And we were always up for a good prank.

Once, after hearing about Nagy's endless negotiations with several computer companies to get the absolute rock-bottom prices when he reoutfitted his investment office with twenty desktops, we couldn't help ourselves. We snuck into his office after his computers had been delivered and removed the ball at the base of every new mouse. When Nagy arrived the next day, he went ballistic, phoning the computer company and screaming, "My mice have no balls!"

We were like college kids having the time of our lives without a notion of the technical revolution that lay ahead: the Internet.

Like any curious kid, I started to wonder what we could do with the computer. My college internship at Channel 10 in San Diego had opened my eyes to how a computer could access information in seconds. But, hard as this is to believe for many college students now, when I came to work with Tim in 1993 most people still didn't have cell phones. People used pagers back then. If a businessman was on the road, he could see the number of the person trying to contact him, and he might stop at a pay phone to return the call. Back then, if you wanted to research a topic you reached for the bound volumes of *Encyclopedia Britannica* that lined libraries and bookshelves across America. Before 1995, there was no such thing as Internet Explorer or Netscape Navigator for people to link up with the Internet. And even when the two Web browsers got up and running in 1995 and gained popularity in 1996, traditional companies like American Express were still living in the past, putting out slick brochures that listed prices on excursions months and maybe even a year in advance.

The future started appearing to me in fragments. At a conference in Chicago run by SABRE, the computer system that American Airlines used to tap into the industry rates, I heard the founder of Netscape speak and immediately realized that information available only to travel agents would soon be accessible to anyone who owned a computer. If our company started a Web site, I figured, we could create a brochure that could be continually updated.

This would allow us to make two major breakthroughs. We could raise or lower our prices in an instant based on demand. Also, we could show our customers rooms offered at our hotels and quickly update the pictures if the rooms were recently refurbished. This might not have been a big deal if we were only selling rooms at the Hilton. A room at the Hilton is a room at the Hilton whether it's in Birmingham or Chicago. But *we* were selling rooms in Las Vegas. The hotels we were offering had exotic themes. People were curious about the pirate motif at Treasure Island, the pyramid designs at the Luxor, and the medieval décor at Excalibur.

When we first launched a rudimentary site in 1996, feedback was immediate. Customers loved seeing pictures of the hotels and discovering the amenities on the properties. The computer screen was much more compelling and efficient than a reservation agent. An agent could only describe the hotels. An agent could pass on rates only as fast as the customer could write them down. Now, in the snap of a finger, the customer's eye could take in columns of rates listed on our site.

It was a huge leap. But our initial Web site was still no more than an electronic brochure. Once the customer saw it, he or she then had to call our 800 number to make the reservation.

Then came an ordinary phone call that nobody would pick up. No matter how many people we hired to work the phones, we never seemed to be able to keep pace with the ringing telephones. Many times, I would jump in and lend a hand, but that would drive Tim crazy.

"Tom, what are you picking up the phone for? That's not your job. You're *in charge* of the company!"

But I just couldn't help myself. If somebody was calling up for our business, I couldn't bear to stand by and let the phone ring. One day, I picked up and, in the best spirit of my mother, got into a conversation with the customer.

"When are we going to be able to book over the Internet," he asked, "without making a phone call?"

I didn't have an answer. So I started to answer more calls. I asked everyone if they'd prefer to book their reservations over the Internet from start to finish. Many said they would. Then I examined all of our e-mails. People were asking about full Internet service there, too.

Usually, I'm the brake and Tim's the accelerator. But I just felt like I had to hit the gas pedal on this one. Still, it wasn't in my nature to go roaring ahead without talking it over.

In October of 1997, Tim and I went to the Notre Dame-USC football game with the Fertittas. Lorenzo's dad was old school and didn't understand or appreciate the Internet at the time. But we really valued his wisdom and counsel. He'd come to Las Vegas from Texas in 1960 with $160 in his pocket and built a multibillion dollar company of casinos that were favorites among the locals. His sons, Frank and Lorenzo, had bought a huge piece of LVRS when Tim needed money at the outset. And they later sold it back to us when LVRS became an impediment to Station Casinos going public. The Fertittas were always there for us.

I explained the possibilities of the Internet to Mr. Fertitta on the ride back from the game. "It might be a great opportunity," he said. "Just don't put yourself in a position where you'll go out of business if it doesn't work. Put half of this year's profit in it and give it a real shot. If it doesn't work, it won't bury you."

I was off and running, and it was a good thing. Because business was changing so fast during those days that a couple of weeks meant the difference between becoming the industry leader with a powerful foothold and a Johnny-come-lately that was lost in the pack.

I sketched out an easy-to-use reservation process with Richie Rich that would take five clicks or less. I wanted each page to load in just a few seconds. Being the fastest travel Web site was important.

Five months and $11,000 later, on February 26, 1998, we launched.

When I came into the office the next day, there was a long queue of reservations listed on the screen. Next to each one was a single word. Charge.

That meant all we had to do was hit a key and the customer's credit card account would be charged.

This six-letter word dropped in a column all the way down the screen.

Charge.

Charge.

Charge.

Charge.

Charge.

Charge.

Charge.

I hit the Charge key and thirty seconds later a message came back from the credit card company indicating the transaction had been approved. I moved on to the next reservation and again hit the Charge key. Thirty seconds later, that one was approved. I sat down and kept hitting the Charge key over and over. It was like money falling from the heavens. All you had to do was hit a key.

I couldn't hit the key fast enough. The queue of reservations was so long I could never catch up—and it was constantly getting longer. I stayed up all night hitting the Charge key.

When he saw what I was doing, Tim's jaw dropped. By the time he picked it up, he already understood the enormity of what had just taken place.

"Tom," he roared, "we can hire somebody else to hit the Charge key! Quick! Let's get some more rooms!"

Neither one of us could sleep. I had the system automated so that we didn't even have to hit the Charge key at all and then went out to hustle up accommodations. If my foot was on the gas, Tim's was pushing the pedal through the floorboards. Search engines like Yahoo, Infoseek, Excite, Lycos, and Alta Vista were now becoming popular. Tim started buying every Las Vegas–based keyword he could get his hands on—even with misspellings of the words "Las Vegas."

"Every quarter we put in," Tim howled, "comes back dressed up as a dollar!"

We were no longer in that place where when you think you've got the best of it, you take dead aim and hold onto your balls. We were now like gamblers at a craps table who knew that every first roll of the dice would come up seven. Tim was pushing all our chips out on the table. Not only that, but he was frantic to get more chips so we could move to a table with higher limits.

"Tom, this doesn't just work for Las Vegas," he said. "It'll work for hotels all around America. It'll work for the entire world!"

"Let's go for it," I said.

A new company was formed. We decided to call it Travelscape.

"I gotta go see Lorenzo," Tim said, bolting out the door.

Once again, Lorenzo was there for us. He loved the idea, and when he bought 10 percent of the company we had an infusion of cash.

But we were growing so fast we needed much more. The beauty of being connected in Las Vegas is there's always a chance you'll find it. When Tim told Uncle Jack about our situation, Uncle Jack made a suggestion. Uncle Jack could always be counted on to come up with money even if it was passed along in unusual ways. When Tim was in college and running low on funds, Uncle Jack sent money through a bookmaker in L.A. known as The Roadrunner. The Roadrunner lived in a huge apartment building, but he wouldn't let Tim come through the doorman to make a quick pickup. The Roadrunner thought that might look suspicious. Instead, at obscure times, he threw manila envelopes containing cash and clasped tight with string out the window of his high-rise. Tim would stand below waiting, and on some windy days looked like a comical outfielder trying to make a catch as the envelope blew back and forth on the currents and dropped into the hedges below.

This time, Uncle Jack suggested that Tim go see an old friend on the East Coast: The Captain.

Captain John Kassap is the great uncle that everybody wishes they had. A guy who sailed around the world as a young man with the Merchant Marines, who could tell you stories about Shanghai in the '40s, who landed in Baltimore, bought a bar, ran junkets to Las Vegas, and over time evolved into an investment guru who could keep up with the sharpest minds at Goldman Sachs. The Captain had no airs, and walked around in a cab driver's cap. His investment record was so good over decades that friends of his put money into projects simply because The Captain recommended them. On the surface, The Captain was not the best candidate to fund a fledgling Internet travel company. He was approaching seventy, and he didn't know anything about computers. To this day, he does his spreadsheets in pencil. And he's not the type to invest over the long haul. No quarterly interest payments for The Captain and his investors. Oh, no. "Me and my guys don't buy green bananas," he liked to say. "We want our interest payments monthly."

But The Captain immediately intuited that travel and the Internet were a perfect partnership. He invited Tim to make a presentation to a group of his pals in Baltimore.

When Tim told Lorenzo that he was going to Baltimore to raise money, Lorenzo's eyelids lifted. *Baltimore?* Lorenzo had been to the dance before when his own company went public back in 1993. He knew how the game was played. You give your pitch at a meeting in New York with investment bankers who'll do their due diligence, who'll make twenty additional phone calls with plenty of questions, and then, if they like the deal, will start negotiating the terms.

Things were a little different in Baltimore. Tim and Lorenzo stepped into a banquet room at a restaurant on the waterfront. There were about thirty guys eating and drinking. Tim went up to the podium and gave his PowerPoint presentation. As soon as he was done, before a single question could be asked, The Captain grabbed the microphone, looked out into the crowd, and said, "All right, now, listen to me! I'm passing around a clipboard. I want you all to write your name down and how much you're in for—and don't embarrass yourself!"

As the evening wound down, Lorenzo stood by in disbelief as people came up to Tim and said, "Oh, I remember going to the racetrack with your Uncle Jack back in . . . must've been 1949. If you're okay with The Captain, you're okay with me, kid. You need money, you can have whatever you need."

After it was over, the bill came to Tim. "Twelve thousand dollars!" he yelped.

"So my guys had a few glasses of wine," The Captain said. "What are you complaining about? We just raised $8 million. Just sign the damn check."

That $8 million built up our infrastructure and propelled our numbers through the roof. In a single year, our sales climbed 60 percent.

The year before the Internet, 1997: $12 million.

The year of the Internet, 1998: $20 million.

Once again, our timing was perfect. The entire travel agency business was being flipped upside down by the Internet. At first, United Airlines cut the standard airline commission to travel agencies from 10 percent down to 8 percent. The other airlines followed suit, and soon commissions were slashed to 5 percent. Then down to $20 maximum per ticket. Eventually, they were cut to nothing at all.

Brick-and-mortar travel agencies with fixed costs that relied on traffic off the streets and phone calls just couldn't compete with five clicks on a computer. We were like the telegraph in the day of the Pony Express. Two days after the last telegraph wire was strung, the Pony Express went out of business.

We threw millions into advertising with search engines and partners. And even with so many reservations coming through the Internet, our phone traffic *tripled*.

We hired Mr. *In*-credible—Edward Muncey—away from the Bellagio to bring in hotel rooms around the country. We'd set a goal. Twenty-five cities and 250 hotels.

"How ya doin', Edward?"

"*In*-credible!" he'd say.

We'd set a new goal. Fifty cities and 500 hotels.

"How ya doin', Edward?"

"*In*-credible!"

A hundred cities and 2,500 hotels.

"How ya doin', Edward?"

"*In*-credible!"

Our revenues shot to the heavens.

The ringing phone that I'd casually picked up in Tim's tiny office back in the days when I was trying to be the next Bob Costas had led to $20 million in revenues by 1998.

By 1999, the revenues that had grown out of the sandwich that Tim bought me on the day we first met reached $100 million.

CHAPTER 5

ARE YOU READY FOR THIS?

If you're going to be David in an arena of Goliaths, you'd better have some rocks for your slingshot.

We were no longer a niche company selling hotel rooms in Las Vegas. We were now a travel company competing in a global market against others run by giants like Microsoft, AOL, and American Airlines. We needed big-time cash. The $8 million dinner with The Captain in Baltimore was great. But now it was time to go to Wall Street.

When I first traveled to New York City just out of college to catch the Big East basketball tournament with Tim, Uncle Jack, and their pals, they loved seeing my head swivel between skyscrapers so they could tease. "Get your head out of the clouds, ya hayseed!" But the reality is that Tim had had a similar sort of experience only a few years earlier. Once, during his college years, he took a trip to New York City with Lorenzo and Lorenzo's mom. The Fertittas booked a hotel room for Tim where they were staying—although Tim insisted upon paying his own way. When Tim checked in at the front desk of the Peninsula, he glanced at the bill and assumed it meant he was supposed to take the elevator to room 375. He asked the clerk, just to make sure, and was informed that 375 was the daily room rate. This was back in the day when $375 was like $675 would be to a college kid now. It was an amount that Tim didn't have, and he couldn't hold back a gasp.

More than a decade had passed since that day. We were now in the summer of 1999. Our company was growing fast. We were young and gung ho. And we couldn't help but feel we belonged in the big time. It's every entrepreneur's dream to go public and see his company listed on the stock exchange. We were embracing the dream. We were such novices to the world of Wall Street that we were too naïve to even realize it.

Fortunately, we had The Captain to look out for us. He came through immediately in a meeting with Goldman Sachs. There's a cachet to doing business with Goldman Sachs. You might have to pay a little more, but it's often worth it to associate your company with the gold standard. The terms that Goldman Sachs was offering, though, were ridiculously loaded down with fees.

"Good morning," the executive at Goldman Sachs cordially greeted Tim and The Captain.

"Good morning???" The Captain shot back at the banker. "With the terms you guys are offering, I don't know what the hell is so good about it!"

If Tim or I had voiced the same opinion, we might've been pitched out to the sidewalk on our thirty-something asses. But having the words come from a guy who'd been to Shanghai and back before the banker was even born gave them credibility.

When Tim and I got in way over our heads, we could always count on The Captain to guide us.

Trouble was, we were navigating our way through a time period that nobody—and I mean *nobody*—could understand. Most people remember the time as the Internet Bubble, though the guy who looked after our finances, Ed Borgato, called it something else. He called it The Crazy.

He called it The Crazy not only because the numbers on Wall Street were insane in early 1999, but also because in a normal world the idea behind running a business is to make a profit. During The Crazy, all you needed to make millions was an idea in a garage. Any young entrepreneur in a T-shirt could float up an Internet concept, and immediately the scent of money was wafting over Wall Street. None of the suits wanted to be left out of the future. Never mind that the company connected to the idea coming from the genius in a T-shirt might have little chance of success. To many of the bankers on Wall Street, it seemed like more of a risk to be left behind.

A big-time analyst like Oppenheimer's Henry Blodget would make an outrageous assessment of a youngster like Amazon.com, predicting in December 1998 that its stock would hit $400 a share. A month later, after a feeding frenzy of investment, the stock had soared 128 percent, and it *did* pass $400! When Amazon grew in leaps and bounds, it spread hope that every company would do the same. It *was* crazy. Without showing a hint of ever having been profitable, an online procurement company called PurchasePro that was started by a guy who showed Steve Wynn workout techniques actually surpassed the value of Wynn's Mirage!

I guess you could compare it to an untested athlete out of high school getting drafted and signed for way more money than a professional who'd proven himself as an all-star for a decade.

The kid out of high school had the power to shape the future. The kid wearing a T-shirt in a garage suddenly had enough money to buy a mansion in Silicon Valley and an original copy of the Declaration of Independence.

Only time can provide true perspective of what we were living through. Hundeds of books have been written about the Internet Bubble, but as I look back now it still boggles the mind. The dot-com valuations were so out of whack during this speculative frenzy that seven years later the NASDAQ Composite would have to appreciate 105 percent to climb back to where it was at the height of The Crazy. Ed watched in disbelief as companies that had nothing to do with the Internet sent their stock climbing simply by changing their names to include a dot-com at the end. Again and again, he issued warnings in his quarterly letter to investors that a day of reckoning was coming. But amateur investors were becoming instant millionaires, and even the savvy were seduced. At the height of the hysteria, Ed wondered how The Crazy could get any crazier. He picked up a business magazine and found out. Barbra Streisand had jumped into The Crazy and was now making a fortune herself as a day trader of Internet stocks. At first, Ed could only shake his head in ridicule when he read that the diva was buying the same stocks that he was shunning. But when he reached the part where fashion designer Donna Karan had pushed aside her money manager and turned to Barbra, he actually hurled the magazine across his office and into the trash.

Ed saw the Internet Bubble for what it was: a new type of gold rush. Wall Street was simply sifting through the different ideas and companies to find the ones with real value. Like in any gold rush, the people who are sure to get rich are the ones selling the picks and the shovels. It was lucrative for Wall Street when an analyst like Henry Blodget dreamed up and affixed an astronomical value to Amazon or any other Internet company. The higher the value, the greater the fee his bank would collect when it launched an initial public offering.

So it was both the best time to go public and the worst. Hundreds of millions of dollars were being handed out on Wall Street as casually as drinks at a bar. Just get in line. If you owned any sort of company linked to the Internet during The Crazy, you were insane if you *didn't* go public. But there would be consequences for those companies that couldn't produce later on, not to mention for the people who'd invested in them.

All the old rules of business were changed overnight by the Internet. Value was no longer based on performance in the present, but on potential performance in the distant future. This was a little complicated for us. Our company was founded *before* the Internet. We were more than just an idea in a garage. We were an actual business that was using the Internet to sell rooms. So we had to understand how Wall Street's new rules varied from the old and how they might affect us.

The concept that the bankers put forth made sense. Yet at the same time it went against everything I always thought a business was supposed to do. How much money your company was making no longer mattered. You were not being judged upon a multiple of your earnings. The analysts wanted the Internet companies that they were taking public to spend so much on marketing that they couldn't possibly make money. The important thing was to use that marketing money to make your company the leader in its niche. In the short term, there would be losses. But when your company became wildly popular, the initial marketing costs would subside. Down the road, your company would reap enormous profits.

In January 1999, Tim and Captain John sat down with vice

presidents from CIBC Oppenheimer. Blodget, the bank's big-time analyst, valued the company that Tim had started with a desk, a chair, a phone, and a pillow at $400 million.

We knew Blodget's numbers were crazy, but if he was willing to give us this sort of valuation, how could we not take it? During The Crazy, you could only wonder if a bank down the street would come up with a figure that was even crazier.

"What the hell," Captain John said to Tim. "Let's walk down the street and listen to Prudential." There, Tim and Captain John heard that our company was worth only $200 million. "Holy mackerel," Captain John said, "we just lost $200 million walking down the street."

When Tim told Prudential about our $400 million valuation, the guy at Prudential threw up its hands. "Whoa, wait a minute, don't do anything yet. Let me talk to *our* analyst. He's in the Far East." Next thing Tim knew, a ringing phone woke him at 3:30 AM. After quickly sharpening his pencil, the analyst in Asia apologized for overlooking certain aspects of our business, and corrected the valuation to $350 million.

"Are you ready for this?" Tim told us the next morning.

"One phone call," Captain John marveled, "and we found $150 million!"

We decided to go with CIBC Oppenheimer and a second-tier bank, Piper Jaffray. The highest number usually won during The Crazy, and we liked Oppenheimer's vice-chairman, Nate Gantcher. Nate seemed at home when he visited us in Las Vegas. Our rottweiler, Bally, had taken a nap with her head on Nate's shoe during a talk in our office. Moments like those meant something to Tim and me. Even when Blodget was lured away by a rival bank and replaced by a young guy who seemed a little jittery in his presentations, we stuck with Nate. We'd shaken Nate's hand. Once we'd given our word, we'd never go back on it. In the city that grew up outside the law, a man's word is all he's worth.

But in the end, the loss of Blodget was a blow. Things became even more complicated when the market grew choppy. The pressure was on Tim when he headed east toward New York and over to Europe to help the bank raise funds for the IPO.

Lorenzo's brother, Frank, told Tim if he wanted to go up against the Goliaths, he needed to look the part. "Request a private plane from the banks in order to help arrange financing," Frank advised. "That will make them take you seriously. The trip is going to be grueling. Ask the banks to load the plane up with whatever you need to make the trip as comfortable as you can." Tim flew off on his mission in a Challenger 601 stocked with Johnnie Walker Blue and Fruity Pebbles cereal.

I held down the fort in Las Vegas while Tim worked his ass off between bowls of Fruity Pebbles. It's no exaggeration to say he was taking a physical pounding as he crisscrossed the country and flew over to Europe. On a stop in Paris, he stepped out of a limo to make a presentation and put his briefcase down behind the trunk. The driver didn't see him and slammed the trunk door down on his head, knocking him unconscious. Tim woke up and wobbled into the presentation. He spoke with blood running down the back of his neck, drenching the shirt underneath his suit. After weeks of unrelenting sales, he got his end of the job done.

On June 22, 1999, we flew family and friends to New York for a dinner at Sparks steak house to celebrate our impending entrance to the stock market. Not long before the shrimp cocktail was served, though, the next sucker punch arrived. The bankers told us they couldn't get enough orders in their book. Why? One reason was that our company wasn't losing enough money. Sure, we showed great potential. We could anticipate sales growth at

40 to 50 percent. But during The Crazy, that just didn't look as appealing to investors as an *unprofitable* company forecasting sales growth of *200* percent. The bankers wanted us to lower our numbers because, they said, the market had softened.

But then we found out that Piper Jaffray had priced another IPO above its initial range and scheduled it for the following morning, at exactly the same time it was supposed to be doing our IPO. I couldn't believe our bank was taking two companies in the same sector public on the same day. I thought it was total bullshit.

Usually, Tim is the guy to throw the first punch. But when I looked over at him, there was no anger on his face. You know how sometimes you get so tired that you can't sleep? Well, Tim was so mad that he was beyond anger. He had thrown so much of himself into the process that he had no more to give. It was one of those moments when you realize you're powerless and you throw the back of your hand in the air and say, "Whatever."

Seeing that expression on Tim's face hit me in the gut with a force that I still can't describe. Suddenly, I was in a rage at the bankers in the dining room of Sparks, and Tim was holding *me* back on the same ground where Big Paulie Castellano was gunned down by John Gotti's boys in one of the last notorious mob hits.

It was completely out of character for me to lose it like that. When I look back on it, I can only wonder if the bankers had tapped into that old high school wound. *You're not playing.* That's pretty much what the bankers were telling us that night. After all their bullshit about how great our company was and how great this offering was going to be, after all the work that Tim had put into raising money, the whole thing came down to almost the exact same words. We're going with somebody else. You're not playing.

It wasn't like I was standing there seeing a movie flashback of myself as a dejected kid in high school. Or a flashback of Tim and me on the frozen lake when he said, "Look, if you come into the business with me, you don't have to rely on other people to create your opportunities. We control our own destiny." The pain behind the blank expression on Tim's face just made me want to beat the crap out of someone.

The bankers started backpedaling, hoping to keep their commission. No, no, they said, you're seeing it all wrong. It's the fluctuations in the market. Just wait two weeks, they insisted, and the time for your IPO will be ripe.

But the game was over. When you walk off a court after the final buzzer, and you haven't played, you can never get that time back.

Tim and I returned to Las Vegas.

It wasn't possible to stay angry or be depressed for long. Word of what happened spread with the wind. Soon it reached the ears of Barry Diller, who knows an opportunity when he smells one. We had to pay attention.

Barry Diller is a billion-dollar American success story. He's the guy who dropped out of UCLA after one semester, started to work in a mail room, went on to invent the made-for-TV movie, and hustled his way up to become chairman of Paramount Pictures. He had a hand in classics like *Saturday Night Fever, Grease,* and *Raiders of the Lost Ark,* and was responsible for the creation of the Fox Broadcasting Company. Diller was also quick to sense the power of the Internet. Over time, he amassed an Internet conglomerate that included Hotel Reservations Network, Home Shopping Network, and Ticketmaster.

Travelscape fit right in his portfolio—and he was willing to pay more than a hundred million bucks for it.

No entrepreneur who starts a business with a desk, a phone,

a chair, and a pillow is going to look away when somebody offers him more than $100 million for it. But there were other reasons to take the money and go on our way. The pace of technology was moving so quickly that even a powerful company like ours could be overwhelmed and replaced in a matter of months. We'd seen it happen all around us.

A classic example is what happened with encyclopedias and the Internet, and how both led to a travel company called Expedia. When Tim and I were in high school and college, we'd go to the twenty-nine-volume *Encyclopedia Britannica* on the library bookshelf to do our research papers. During that time period, Microsoft approached *Encyclopedia Britannica* about an electronic partnership, but the folks at Britannica couldn't see the future. They declined. Microsoft purchased the rights to another reference library called *Funk and Wagnalls*, and in 1993 used its contents to create an electronic encyclopedia on CD-ROM called *Encarta*. The project was run by a guy named Rich Barton, and it was stupendous. Because 90 percent of it was devoted to pictures, movies, and audio clips, it pole-vaulted over anything on a library bookshelf. *Britannica*, an icon that had been published since 1768 and was once described as "beyond comparison because there is no competitor," would in the mid-1990s be sold as a company below book value. Not long thereafter, *Funk and Wagnalls* would stop printing. The first avalanche of the electronic word over the printed word had occurred. The avalanches were only beginning.

Only a year after *Encarta* came out, in 1994 a Web browser called Netscape arrived. Its interface enabled the owners of diverse computers to access this new thing called the Internet. When it did, the *Encarta* CD-ROM was rendered virtually obsolete. Information that you could get by purchasing the CD-ROM was now available on the burgeoning Internet through Netscape.

Only a year before, *Encarta* had looked like a moon landing of technology. Now it suddenly seemed like the Nina, Pinta, and Santa Maria. Netscape was the future. It launched an IPO in 1995 at $28 a share and shot to $75 on the first day of trading. Netscape's new technology allowed Web sites to send weather and stock updates directly to a user's desktop. In the mid-1990s, its user share hovered as high as 85 percent.

This was obviously threatening to Microsoft, which had its own Internet browser called Internet Explorer and a very limited CD-ROM in *Encarta*. Microsoft wanted to see a world with a computer on every desktop and its software in every computer. It wanted people to access the Internet through its own browser: Internet Explorer. It was involved in a multibillion-dollar game of checkers. It leaped over Netscape by packaging Internet Explorer within its software so that it was virtually free. No longer would anybody have to pay Netscape for the privilege to browse the Internet. Suddenly, Netscape was virtually useless. It would sue Microsoft for monopolistic practices and ultimately was sold to America Online. But the dots are easy to connect. By the end of 2006, the usage share of Netscape browsers had fallen to 1 percent. Not only did Microsoft triumph (although it did have to pay Netscape a settlement), it was also smart enough to rethink *Encarta*.

Encarta had a huge geographical component. A page containing information about Mexico could be electronically linked to a site that sold travel south of the border. Ultimately, a huge electronic travel company backed by Microsoft would be spun out of this connection. That company would be called Expedia.

The point is that if you weren't on the cutting edge, or flush with a lot of money to reformat quickly, you were very vulnerable to the next technological avalanche. Barry Diller was offering to pay us $120 million to remove that vulnerability.

Neither Tim nor I had met Diller when he offered to buy Travelscape. At first, he sent in a team of people to study our company. That's fairly common. If you want to buy a company valued at more than a hundred million bucks you want to know exactly what you're getting.

But Diller owned our top competitor: Hotel Reservations Network.

Opening your books to your main rival never sits well in your stomach. Especially when the weasel-of-a-lawyer asking you questions over lunch is the type to throw his tie over his shoulder before he bites into a sandwich so he doesn't stain it with ketchup. Those lunches were just creepy. Some of our employees, who'd met the people at the company they'd be merging with, were not particularly comfortable, either. They never came out and said so directly, but an uneasy spirit hovered over the office—a spirit that we were too busy to recognize and address. We were working eighteen hours a day, moving through the Diller deal, and handling the company's day-to-day operations. So alarm bells didn't go off when we asked Mr. *Incredible* "How ya doin', Edward?"

And he responded "Okay."

But that's what happens when you're being pulled in too many directions. The whole process felt like the sort of investigation you get when you apply for a gaming license in Nevada—and that has been described as a visit to the proctologist.

Our negotiations with Diller went on for three months and got down to the paperclips. Finally, everything was set. Diller offered us $120 million for the company. On a Thursday, we were supposed to fly to New York and have dinner with him. On Friday, we'd sign the contract.

Less than twenty-four hours before we were to board the plane, Tim got a phone call from one of Diller's representatives.

I couldn't hear the whole conversation. I could only pick up what was going on from Tim's responses and his facial expressions. But it's not difficult to get the gist of a punch to the gut.

"Our board is having second thoughts," said Diller's rep. "It thinks the valuation is too high. And it's not going to vote for the deal. It's offering $90 million—less your company's $8 million debt."

"What kind of bullshit is this?" Tim said. "You get me pregnant on the idea of selling and then at the last minute you're gonna haircut it?"

"I don't want you to think this is intentional. I know you're upset. You have every right to be. It's not me. It's the board."

"Look, we made a deal for $120 million. And as far as I'm concerned, a deal is a deal."

"But the board won't vote for that deal."

"Well, then, fuck it. We don't got a deal."

"Look, just think about—"

"There's nothing to think about. We went through three months of due diligence in good faith. You gave me your word. A deal is a deal."

"Look, Tim, $82 million is a lot of money."

"Yeah, and the $38 million that you fucked us out of is a lot of money, too."

Tim's words lifted me right out of my chair. My fist cut through the air, and I was screaming "That's right!" without any sound coming out of my mouth.

"Just think about it overnight," Diller's rep tried to soothe Tim, "and we'll talk in the morning."

"No, we won't," Tim fired back. "Unless you tell me right now, on this phone call, that we have the $120 million that we agreed on, we got no deal. I'm not sleeping on it. I'm not calling you back. I'm not gonna try to calm myself down. This is it. Either it's $120 million on this phone call or don't call me back."

"Tim, I'm not authorized to give you that deal."

"Well, then we got no deal!"

Then Tim slammed down the phone.

The earth seemed to pause. Tim and I stared at each other in silence and thought, "What the fuck just happened?"

"I think," Tim finally said, "we just blew the deal."

Our disbelief turned to devastation. For three months, we'd handed over nearly every scrap of company information to a top competitor. Now we had nothing, and we were numb.

But it was only a minute or two before our blood was flowing again. "Fuck 'em! We'll just roll up our sleeves and make this company bigger than ever."

While we were lifting ourselves out of the muck, the phone rang. It was Diller's rep.

We just let it ring . . . and ring . . . and ring.

It wasn't until years later that we found out what was going on at the other end of that phone line.

Tim didn't know it, but he was on speakerphone. Diller, members of his board, and some bankers were listening to Tim's every word.

Diller didn't think we'd have the balls to turn him down. He's a deal junkie, and he was taking a shot at us, knowing that a lot of guys in our situation would've been happy to be set for life.

"Yeah, we want the deal," Diller had told the room before the call. "But these guys are young. Trust me, they'll take $82 million."

Even after Tim hung up in fury, Diller said, "Don't worry. He'll call back."

The call became famous among some of Diller's bankers

because Tim was the only guy they knew who'd told Barry Diller to go fuck himself.

Twice within six months we'd gotten to the goal line only to be repelled just before we could score. Little did we know that the failed IPO and the Diller debacle were preparing us for what was coming our way, way down the road. I suppose you can rationalize what Diller did to us with motivational quotations. As Henry Ford once said, "Remember, that the airplane takes off against the wind, not with it."

But as we turned off the lights and closed the door to Tim's office that night, we felt like we were moving in slow motion. We headed home exhausted and beaten men.

CHAPTER 6

SMASHING THROUGH

After the beating we'd just taken, the last company you'd think we'd want to see on the opposite side of a negotiating table would be Microsoft. That would be kind of like a fighter getting flattened by the number nine contender, then the number ten contender, then getting up, rubbing his jaw, and saying, "Bring on the champ!"

Microsoft had not only squashed Netscape. It was rolling over nearly every company in its path on its quest to dominate the software market. If a rival with an innovative product wouldn't sell out to Microsoft, there was no mercy. Microsoft simply built a replica into the next version of its own software and made the competitor irrelevant—which is one reason it was being sued for monopolistic tactics by individual companies, twenty states, and the U.S. government.

But we had something that couldn't be replicated by a software developer at three in the morning behind beads hanging over an open doorway on Microsoft/Expedia's sacred fifth floor in Redmond, Washington. We had the relationships in Las Vegas and a lock on the rooms. We were selling two million a year, and it would cost Microsoft millions of dollars and years of effort to duplicate that.

We also had a friendly history with Microsoft. For years, we'd made each other money. Early on, we bought advertising space on the travel page of Microsoft's Internet portal, MSN.com, and the hotel page on Expedia.com. At the same time, we sold a lot of hotel rooms when November came around for the Comdex Expo in Las Vegas, a platform Microsoft liked to use to launch its products. Comdex was the one of the largest computer conferences in the world at the time and seemed to take place under Microsoft's shadow. The company actually rented out the entire Mirage for its employees, who all walked around in khaki pants and blue shirts. The first time Tim saw these guys, he turned to me and said, "And I thought *you* were a square!" But we had to respect what they'd created. Thousands flew in from around the world to hear Bill Gates give the keynote address at the conference, and we had the room receipts to prove it.

So we were actually in a good position when we began to talk to Rich Barton about selling Travelscape to Expedia. We had a solid relationship. We were now war tested. We had a cash offer from American Express for $100 million in our back pocket. And soon after the Diller debacle we'd brought in a chief operating officer who could walk among the Goliaths.

Steve Cavallaro had worked for large outfits like Harrah's and run the Fertittas' Palace Station. He didn't have a nickname, but I call him The Sniffer because it didn't take him long to sniff out employees like The Weasel and The Floater, and weed out others who didn't do much and were great at camouflaging it. He scrutinized deals we'd made with distributors and renegotiated them in our favor. He was the type of guy who could be counted on to dot every *i* and cross every *t* in a negotiation with Microsoft.

Everything Tim and I had been through during the failed IPO and the negotiations with Diller had changed our outlook on doing a deal. In a negotiation, everybody knows you're not supposed to throw out the first number. Why ask for $105 million if the person you're making a deal with is prepared to give you $200 million? But our recent experiences had taught us otherwise. It was ironic that some people saw Tim as a Vegas slickster. Tim was merely looking for someone he could trust. "Look," Tim told Barton, "we'll sell you Travelscape for $105 million in Expedia stock. It's not our first number. It's our last number. So if you don't like the deal, let's just forget about it. We won't waste your time and you won't waste ours. We're not negotiating. A hundred and five million in Expedia stock means a hundred and five million in Expedia stock. That's the number."

Barton immediately recognized the deal's potential. Expedia had airline contracts, distribution, and technology mastered. We had a huge customer base and a great hotel inventory built around the merchant model. It's hard to imagine now, but back then you couldn't choose from a full range of hotel *and* airline options on a single Internet site or build your own vacation package. A synergy of Expedia and Travelscape gave the world access to Expedia's airlines and our hotels. It was like introducing french fries to a hamburger. Barton could readily see that the two companies combined were worth way more than they were independently. It was one of those deals where 1 + 1 = 50.

We began to work the details out with Rich. The Sniffer spent a few weeks dotting every *i* and crossing every *t*. We were all set to go. Then, just as we prepared to fly up to Seattle to close the deal, Tim got a terrible case of the flu. You can imagine how sick he was to stay in bed. But executives at Expedia couldn't. They saw it as a negotiating ploy, and they didn't bring Barton to the table.

The Sniffer, two lawyers, and I walked toward a conference room in the law offices of Bill Gates's father, past hundreds of boxes reading: U.S. Government vs. Microsoft. That will get you thinking.

About twelve guys from Microsoft sat at the conference table behind laptops as we tried to wrap up the final half-dozen points of the deal. It seemed like we were making good progress through a long day of work. Late in the afternoon, we took a break. When we returned, one of their lawyers started leading the meeting as if we'd never been in the same room.

It was as if we'd left for the break on the one-yard line, about to punch it in for a score, and returned to find ourselves starting at the fifty and moving in slow motion. "Let's go back to these points," they'd say in the most methodical way. Was this the same old story? They get the carrot halfway in your mouth and out comes the bulldozer. Or was it the genius of Microsoft? They just wear you down. It was hard to know. You couldn't even look these guys in the eyes. They were hunched over, concealed by their laptops.

Either way, The Sniffer was in a state of utter disbelief. He'd been in all kinds of big deals. He knew the routine. Everybody throws down a line in the sand. But compromises are always reached at the end. And when you're buying a company from someone who started it and has deep emotional ties, you've got to do some serious massaging. Look the owner in the eye. Give on some points. Make the owner feel good.

All we could see was the bulldozer's steel plate heading straight for us.

The Sniffer slammed his hand on the table. "You're making no compromises whatsoever," he said. "You guys don't know how to get a deal done. I'm gonna recommend to Tim and Tom that we take a different deal." Then he walked out.

I sat in silence for about thirty seconds. I didn't quite know what to do. It was the first time I'd ever been in a negotiation like this. Sure, I'd haggled over hotel room rates with our suppliers. But this was on a different level. Our attorney, Peter Wallace, took charge. "We're going to take a break, and we'll let you know how to proceed."

We met The Sniffer outside. He'd seen it for what it was. The Microsoft culture was used to rolling over everybody across the table, and we were across the table. It's not every day you blow a $100 million. This was the third time in less than a year that a nine-figure deal had slipped through our fingers.

We phoned Tim. "Are you ready for this?"

Tim was right behind us. We left a message with Expedia that we were headed back to our hotel.

Over dinner at the hotel, the phone rang. It was Expedia's chief financial officer, Greg Stanger. "Where are you guys?" he said. "We're all sitting in the conference room waiting to resume talks."

The Sniffer and the lawyer were writing notes on my napkin, advising me what to say. I gleaned the information, but then there was a moment when I stopped reading, looked up, and became somebody who I wasn't only a half hour before.

"We're trying to get a deal done here," Stanger said.

"You guys know what the issues are." My tone was straightforward and completely reasonable. "When you're prepared to compromise, let me know. If I don't hear from you by early tomorrow morning, we're leaving at eight thirty."

That night, I set my cell phone on the nightstand. Nothing. I tossed, turned, and woke up every two hours. Nothing. We headed to the airport the following morning. As we boarded the plane, my stomach felt as lousy as it could possibly feel without throwing up. I remember flying over Mount Rainier. It was a picturesque day. The Sniffer and the lawyers were trying to cheer me up, but I could barely hear a word they were saying. The detail I most remember about the ride is there was no turbulence.

When we landed, there was a message on my phone to call Tim. I dialed him immediately. "Where are you?" he asked.

"We just landed in Vegas."

"Vegas! What are you doing in Vegas?" he said. "You've got to be up in Seattle to sign the contract!"

He was joking—and not joking. While we were in the air, he'd spoken to Rich Barton over the phone and ironed out the deal.

There was high-fiving and hugging and of course Tim couldn't resist a few digs. "What I *forgot* about doin' deals, most people never knew!" Joe Pesci couldn't have executed it any better. Only years later, after I'd met Tony and Danny Bennett, did I fully understand that I'd played an integral role in making the deal. At the time, I was just overjoyed it was done.

The deal was announced on January 31, 2000, the day after the Super Bowl. Tim and I had sold Travelscape for $105 million in Expedia stock. People have asked what it's like to make a hundred-million-dollar deal. All I can say is that the feeling really didn't hit until I saw the stock certificate months later.

What I do remember from that time is a moment that came

up when lawyers began to sort through the paperwork. They asked Tim and me for a document that showed our fifty-fifty split of the company. We had nothing to hand them. We'd never written one up.

"You mean," the lawyers asked, "you don't have anything on paper proving your partnership in the company?"

It was impossible for them to believe that all we had, that all we needed, was a handshake on a frozen lake.

If all this sounds like a fairy tale, read on. Only a couple of months after we'd sold our company to Expedia, the Internet Bubble burst. Wall Street had finally realized that most of the tech companies were more concept than viable businesses, and there was a stampede for cover. Even investors who could see the fall coming were surprised by its severity. As the market bottomed out, companies formerly valued in the billions were suddenly declaring bankruptcy. The dot-com millionaires who'd borrowed against their stock to buy Lamborghinis and mansions went bust, and many a bandwagon investor lost everything.

As our Expedia stock skidded lower and lower, there was nothing we could do. We couldn't even sell. The shares we'd received in the deal were restricted from being sold—and the price plummeted before the restriction was lifted. So we simply watched as our stock sank with the rest of the technology market. But when it fell from $34 to $7—and we'd lost $80 million—I couldn't take it anymore. I phoned Ed and blurted "What the fuck is going on? This is crazy!"

"No, Tom," Ed said. "This is the *end* of The Crazy."

Ed tried to calm Tim and me by explaining that The Crazy had little to do with us. There was simply no correlation between the way Expedia stock was being priced and the company's true value. Expedia's stock was plummeting only because every dot-com's stock was plummeting. Ed sensed that as worthless

Internet companies crashed, genuine businesses like Expedia would find a base and recover. Forget about the numbers on the stock market, he advised us. Look at Expedia's sales. When I looked closely I began to relax. The addition of Travelscape had bolstered Expedia and sent its revenues soaring. And we're talking about the Microsoft culture, here. This was a company born with a vision of smashing through any wall put in front of it. Now that Expedia had the power of our operation behind it, it was on its way to becoming the largest seller of travel in the world.

Time proved Ed right. Expedia not only recovered, but our shares soared from $7 to $150 by the summer of 2003. When they did, we had more money than when we first signed the deal.

But as clairvoyant as Ed could be, he couldn't fathom where the sale of Travelscape would take our day-to-day lives. Neither could Tim. And neither could I. Looking back on it, these changes were much more profound than the dive and soar in the stock market.

As part of the deal with Expedia, I began overseeing staff and implementing the global hotel strategy as the two companies came together. I wanted to make sure that the transition was smooth for all the people who'd worked so hard for Tim and me at Travelscape. No way was I taking my money and running off to retire in the Land of Grey Goose. It was an important time for me. No matter how hard I'd worked and contributed to build Travelscape, I knew damn well that it had been Tim's inspiration. I needed to find out if I truly belonged at a conference table with the likes of men who ran billion-dollar businesses. So I opened myself up to learning as much as I could. And you know what? It was great. I was traveling to Europe frequently and setting up Expedia offices in London, Munich, and Paris.

After years of working sixteen hours a day, I opened myself up to a social life. Let me tell you, going out with Miss Israel at that time would've opened anybody's mind. Miss Israel of 1999, Rana Raslan, is Palestinian. I was a long way from Barnsville.

My eyes were wide to the new world in front of me. Because of that I didn't see the deep funk that Tim was sliding into. Tim didn't know what to do when he got up in the morning. Yeah, he was doing some consulting for Expedia, but his role was more detached. Most days, he had nowhere to go and nobody to see. He might have stayed in bed all day if the housekeeper didn't arrive at eight thirty every morning. Being in bed when she arrived made him feel like a loser. So he showered, dressed, and got behind the wheel of his Mercedes without any idea where he was going. Sometimes he went out for breakfast. Sometimes he went to a bookstore. Many afternoons he sat alone through a matinee. For a little while he forced himself to go out at night and act like a playboy. But that wasn't him, and he knew it.

He tried to make sense of his funk by looking at the lives of Bill Clinton and Steve Wynn. He wondered what Clinton would do at a relatively young age now that the presidency was behind him. And now that Wynn had just sold more than two decades of his creativity and relentless work on The Golden Nugget, the Mirage, Treasure Island, and the Bellagio to Kirk Kerkorian and MGM, what new ground would Steve break?

Everything Tim had done, everything he was, pointed back to his business. Now he felt like he'd given up his baby. He missed everything about it. It was more than driving hard for bigger numbers and celebrating over T-bones and cigars at Morton's steak house. Tim missed playing practical jokes on Naaygs. He missed the laughter that rocked the office. Even when he'd gotten into a fistfight with a pediatrician over parking spaces at our ever-expanding office, he might have regretted it later, but he damn well knew he was alive. Pressure, tension, stress—that's what made Tim's heart tick.

Though he had millions in the bank, Tim felt hollow. His days were no longer filled with Frank Sinatra. Now, he heard Peggy Lee singing "Is That All There Is?" Who could possibly comprehend what he was going through? The kid who had to hope for his dad to make a winning bet the night before a vacation to Disneyland could now provide for his extended family beyond his mother's wildest imagination. There were about fifty million men in America who were wishing for Tim's dilemma. If he so desired, Tim would never have to work another day for the rest of his life. What right did he have to complain?

He didn't tell me or anybody else, but he started seeing a shrink and taking Prozac.

One thing you learn about having a dream come true is that you're going to wake up the following morning. When you do, it's wise to have another dream or goal in place.

I had a goal. I had to see how well I could do on my own. So the transformation after the sale was much easier for me precisely because the questions I needed to answer set a staircase in front of me. One of those steps took me to a seat on Expedia's board of directors in February of 2002, just as Barry Diller bought a 60 percent share of the company from Microsoft. Suddenly, I found myself preparing to sit at the same conference table to work side by side with the guy who'd screwed Tim and me over when we'd tried to sell him Travelscape!

"Is Tom still mad at me?" Diller wanted to know before I joined the board.

There are people who would've refused to enter a room with Diller if he'd done to them what he'd done to us. Make no mistake about that. But Sumner Redstone, the CEO of Viacom, says he doesn't let history get in the way of the future. Anyway, that's just the attitude I took.

That first board meeting with Diller was a big day in my life — one of those days when you're up before the alarm clock rings. Say what you want about the guy, but the list of people who've worked with Diller over the years grabs your lapels and gets your attention. Michael Eisner, who became the CEO of Disney, mentored under Diller. So did Jeffrey Katzenberg, who started DreamWorks with Steven Spielberg. At one point, they called those guys the Killer Dillers. I simply needed to know if I could hold a seat in the room at that level.

I was staying in New York at my favorite hotel, the St. Regis. I put on my best suit. My best shirt. My best tie. Maybe I looked like I belonged in a Barry Diller boardroom. But inside I was still the same guy who had a hard time figuring out trigonometry. The same guy who'd been rejected by his high school basketball coach. The same guy whose dad would be deeply wounded if I ever sacrificed my solid Midwestern values for the almighty buck.

I didn't go out and buy a fancy house as soon as the money became available. I sent some to my parents, who'd given me those solid values. I sent some to my older brothers, who'd probably stunted my growth with all those Piledrivers and helped create my Charlie Hustle attitude. I sent some to my younger brother, John, who is so close to me that we talk five times a day. I sent some to my old backcourt partner Chris Bednarz for helping me learn how to synthesize. I gave some stock to a school that Andre Agassi and Perry Rogers were establishing for inner city kids in Las Vegas. Let me tell you, it's a great a thing to be able to give the Nevada Cancer Institute a million bucks. Well, yeah, I also bought a Ferrari — which gave Tim the perfect opportunity to twist in his needle. "No, Tom, you haven't gotten away from those humble Midwestern roots. You're just driving a *Ferrari!*"

But there was probably nothing $105 million could buy to make me feel as good as the tape I received in the mail from Chris Bednarz's dad not long before that board meeting with Diller. It was a recording of that basketball game against Totino-Grace. The Ferrari is long gone. But that win will always be with me. Now, I needed to know if I could seize the moment like that in Barry Diller's boardroom.

It was about five months after 9/11, and tension from the destruction of the World Trade Center still hung over the city. I stepped out of the street and into the anxiety of the boardroom. Everybody attached to Microsoft was anxious to find out where he or she would fit in now that Expedia would be under Diller's control.

Diller was very cordial. I sat between him and Greg Maffei, the former chief financial officer of Microsoft. I could hear my heart beating as I wondered when to jump into the conversation and how to time my comments so that I didn't sound as long-winded as Tim would have you believe I am.

After that three-and-a-half-hour meeting, I was no longer a kid who'd stepped into an amazing opportunity on a frozen lake still trying to find his way in the world. I knew I belonged at that table, and I was deeply aware of how much I'd changed in a decade.

The changes were confirmed over the next year and a half when Diller bought the remaining 40 percent of Expedia. I was placed on a special committee in charge of negotiating the price with Diller on behalf of Expedia shareholders. It was a tough negotiation. Believe me, Diller ended up paying more than he wanted. But in the end, everyone got a fair deal. And Diller and I sent each other notes wishing each other the best.

Closure always makes it easier to open the next door.

That door was opening now that Tim was emerging from his funk. Once again, Bishop Gorman High School had come through for him.

While depressed and uncertain what to do next, Tim complained to Perry that I wasn't around enough. Perry helped him see the big picture. He explained to Tim that I needed to learn what I was capable of doing on my own. It was the same reason, Perry intuited, that he'd needed to add Shaquille O'Neal to his own business. Otherwise people would've thought that he was successful only because Andre Agassi happened to be his best friend. He had to prove that his success as Andre's agent wasn't luck. He had to prove that to everybody around him. And he had to prove it to himself.

Then Lorenzo invited Tim to join the board of directors at Station Casinos. The board met quite often, and being around gaming began to light a spark inside Tim. That spark began to kindle when he got a call from another Bishop Gorman grad, Curt Magleby, who many years before had learned a lesson in discipline at the blackjack table with Tim at his side.

One day, during their junior year, the water was turned off at Bishop Gorman, and the students were let out early. Tim and Curt went to lunch at the Barbary Coast and then wandered over to the Dunes with about $50. They must've looked at least twenty-one years old when they ran it up to $1,200 on the blackjack table, because they were able to convince the hotel to comp their dinner, as well.

Knowing he'd gotten "the best of it," Tim wanted to leave after dessert. Curt wanted to use the $1,200 as a base to "take the joint down." So they strolled over to a $100 blackjack table and ten minutes later their pockets were empty. Ratcheted between disbelief and fury, Tim headed out the front door, weaved to the fountain out front, and dunked his head in the water as a reminder never again to betray his instincts.

That dunk became more memorable to Curt than any of Michael Jordan's. He went on to become an investment banker who specialized in arranging gaming partnerships and buyouts. When he heard that the longtime owner of the Imperial Palace was in bad health and trying to sell the hotel before he died, he phoned Tim to ask if he'd be interested in buying.

Curt's call was like another slam dunk in a fountain. Tim came up blinking with the realization that he was actually in a position to take a shot at his dream. Curt was an expert on raising money for these investments. If Curt thought Tim was qualified, so would everybody else.

The desire to own a casino was in Tim's DNA. And after we'd been apart for more than a year, what better way was there for Tim to bring back the old magic than to include his best friend?

One day I went to meet Tim at his office. He was poring over a desk covered with spreadsheets. I should have seen it coming.

"Hey, buddy, have you got 25 million bucks?"

CHAPTER 7

SUBSTANCE IS EVERYTHING

You only have to get rich once.

When you understand that, you understand there is absolutely no reason to risk a fortune. Lose it, Ed Borgato will be happy to remind you, and you'll have to make it all over again.

But advice like that has little impact on Tim. That's because, for Tim, life is not really about the money. For Tim, money is only a measurement of how well he's succeeding at his passions. Once Tim thought he could have the best of it owning a casino, he was going to have one. It didn't matter if he needed to put all his chips on the table to get it.

Probably the best way to describe the blood that runs through Tim's veins comes from Jack Binion, who's taken some of the largest bets in the history of Las Vegas at Binion's Horseshoe and who just may be the smartest guy in gambling.

Manufactured emotion—that's what Binion calls gambling.

This is how Binion explains manufactured emotion. Just say you're in college. You're going to USC. When USC plays a basketball game, you've naturally got a rooting interest. Your spirit is in that game. You're screaming for your team, and your heart's pumping when that last-second shot goes up at the buzzer. Now, just say USC doesn't make it to the Final Four. But Georgetown does. You've never gone to Georgetown. You have no attachment to the school whatsoever. But you believe Georgetown is going to win its next game—so you place a large bet on Georgetown. Welcome back, school spirit!

Tim had gotten back the old school spirit, all right. He was even willing to go through the rigors of a gaming license investigation in order to own a casino.

But I've never been a gambler. So the situation looked completely different to me. The idea of working with Tim again definitely gave me a tingle. But Tim was already bounding along the high board and about to take the dive of his dreams. This put me in a strange place—two places, actually. I was with Tim in spirit. At the same time, I was watching him race toward that dive from a detached distance.

Tim was asking me to put up $25 million in an industry that I was still learning about. And when I started asking people in the industry what they thought, many seemed shocked. "What? You want to go back to working like dogs again? Do you know how hard this business is? Especially with a property that needs a lot of work!"

It wasn't the work that made me apprehensive. It was stepping into territory I knew little about. I wrote out pages and pages of questions for Tim. That drove him nuts. When one partner is gunning the gas and the other is hard on the brake, you can get locked up. That's why it's helpful to bring in people you trust to smooth the ride—which is where Perry Rogers and Andre Agassi came in.

Andre and Perry first met when Andre was eleven and Perry was twelve.

Perry had just won a junior doubles title playing alongside Curt Magleby—the same Curt who years later won and quickly lost $1,200 at the blackjack table with Tim at the Dunes, and then watched in amazement as Tim punished himself by dunking his head in the fountain out front.

After Curt and Perry had won their doubles championship match, Perry wandered over to a girl who'd caught his eye. She was cheering for Andre in the single's championship. Turns out she was Andre's sister.

Andre lost his match and was none too pleased when he came off the court. When he saw Perry next to his sister, he asked "Who are you?" in a tone that Perry took to be dismissive. The lingering scent of the remark made Perry want to kick Andre's ass.

Word got around about the affront, and the more it did the more it twisted in Perry's belly. Now, Perry *really* wanted to kick Andre's ass.

The story takes a fork in the road here depending on which of the two is doing the telling. Later that day, Perry got a call to meet Andre at the Red Rock Theater. He thought he was being summoned to duke it out, and he had his mom drive him over. But he arrived late. He entered the theater and walked down the aisle in darkness. There was an open seat next to Andre. When Andre saw Perry, he offered the seat up.

Perry was thinking, "How can you kick the ass of someone who's just saved you a seat?"

The film was a horror movie, and horror movies make Perry queasy. The guy who'd come to kick some ass was now cringing and covering his eyes all through the feature. Afterward, they went to a donut place called Winchell's, where the friendship was sealed during a short conversation between Perry and the guy behind the counter.

"That sign at the door," Perry pointed out, "says you're open twenty-four hours a day."

"That's right," said the guy behind the counter.

"And you're open seven days a week?" Perry asked. "Three hundred and sixty-five days a year?"

"Correct," the guy behind the counter nodded.

"Even holidays?"

"Even holidays."

"Then why," Perry asked, "is there a lock by the front door?"

Something inside Andre screamed, "Whoa!"

He couldn't articulate it then, but he can now. What appealed to him in that moment, he'll tell you twenty-six years later, is Perry's knack for questioning parameters. Why are things this way? Why do these rules apply? Once he saw Perry question boundaries, he began to question boundaries himself. Once he began to ask those sorts of questions, it made him realize that how he responded to the answers could have an impact over whatever situation he found himself in.

Any true friendship comes down to a single word: trust. But the partnership between Perry and Andre functioned a little differently than the one between Tim and me.

If you looked at Tim and me as gas pedal and brake, you might see Andre and Perry as a game of leapfrog. You might even call it leap the lock. Whenever Perry or Andre seemed to be walled in, the two of them could always figure out a way to vault over the wall.

When Perry needed money to go to law school, he asked

Andre for a loan. Andre was doing well as a professional tennis player at that point, but he didn't answer. When Perry asked why, Andre said, "Because you need the money. Why would I need to respond?"

Perry went to law school. But law school classes were not his priority. His mind was focused on setting Andre free.

Andre had been trapped by three words. He was a rising tennis star who hadn't won a Grand Slam tournament when the agency that represented him set up an ad campaign with a camera company. A single television commercial turned Andre's world upside down. It painted one of the most intense people you'll meet into a party boy with flowing hair who seemed to revel in making money off his good looks and flair as opposed to winning tournaments. The commercial framed Andre with a slogan that couldn't have misrepresented him more: Image Is Everything.

Catchy for a camera company. Punishing for a world-class athlete who'd never won a Grand Slam tournament. The image followed Andre like a second shadow and drove him crazy.

Perry set up an office in his room. His law school years became devoted to helping Andre leap over those three words. By the time Perry graduated, Andre had won at Wimbledon. A U.S. Open championship soon followed. Image Is Everything was soon behind them. And Andre's success had leapfrogged Perry to new ground.

Now, Perry was twenty-six years old and negotiating directly with Phil Knight at Nike on what would be one the largest sports marketing deals ever. Perry seized the moment and thought beyond traditional formulas. He didn't want to do the deal in cash. He asked for and received Nike stock, which linked Andre's ascent to the rise of one of the most powerful companies in the world.

The deal took Andre to a place where he'd never have to worry about finances again. It allowed Andre to devote himself to performance. Andre would use that freedom to become one of only five men to win all four Grand Slams. He'd lead the U.S. team to victory in the Davis Cup, win an Olympic gold medal, and capture more ATP Masters tournaments than any other player. He'd earn more than $31 million in prize money. And he'd use that freedom to live a full and complete life.

All of this only widened Perry's horizon. People took note of what Andre and Perry were accomplishing. It wasn't long before Shaquille O'Neal approached Perry and asked if he'd represent him. The partnership with Shaquille expanded Perry's business and led to meetings with new partners that set in motion a hotel deal for Andre in Idaho. Andre became involved in so many deals with Perry that he might actually be in a position as a businessman to leap far beyond what he accomplished as a tennis player.

Perry and Andre's partnership was never about getting the other to a specific location. It was about one making a move so the two of them could advance. After awhile, their movements were so fluid that their simple game of leapfrog had turned into a blur that led to the construction of the Andre Agassi College Preparatory Academy. Now, there are 630 kids from Northwest Las Vegas going to school tuition-free who'll have a chance to play leapfrog with Andre and Perry. Who can possibly have any idea where that will lead?

That's the energy that Tim and I got when Andre and Perry joined us as partners, a force that immediately took Tim and me to new ground.

Perry is the type of guy who surveys the terrain, sets a goal, and then relentlessly pursues it. Andre intuits his way, gets closer and closer to where he needs to go, and then lasers in. Just being around their confidence made me feel comfortable, and added an intensity that Andre compares to surfing a huge wave. When you've got four guys dropping down the face of a wave simultaneously, all of you understand in the same instant what it's like to be in deep, that one misstep will bring the wave crashing down. When everybody can appreciate what everybody else is feeling, it makes the ride that much more exhilarating.

We started to look around for a hotel. Buying a casino is not like going to the store to find a new suit. You're literally buying the clothes off somebody's back. And the guy selling usually doesn't want to undress in public. So the process starts with phone calls that few people know about and continues behind closed doors.

You want to buy a hotel-casino, like any other business, when it's underperforming and you can sense a lot of upside. The Imperial Palace was underperforming all right, and it had a great location on The Strip. But nobody wanted to go out on the town looking like the Imperial Palace. If it were a suit, it would've been ready for the trash bin. As a hotel, it was begging for the wrecking ball.

We turned to the Hard Rock, then to The Golden Nugget. Not for sale, not for sale.

The Las Vegas Hilton was, and it caught our eye. It was a landmark with sixty acres—more of a real estate play, really, but filled with history. Barbra Streisand had headlined in the showroom back in the day. Elvis filled up the joint every night until his death in 1977. The Hilton had recently started to slide when its owner turned its attention toward its newer properties on The Strip. That's what made it a great deal. It was only a block away from the convention center, and it had acres of developable land. It was the land that really gripped Tim. Anybody who's grown up in Vegas has heard somebody older tell tall tales about the amazing increases in land value over the years that aren't really tall tales at all because they're true. Land value appreciates in most places. But in Vegas, property prices have always had the capacity to turn eyes into the size of teacups. "Oh, nobody will ever pay that," people always say. But somebody always does. And when everybody looks back, the price always seems cheap.

The Hilton was a great deal. The asking price was somewhere around $300 million, and it would cost a whole lot more to replicate the towers holding 3,000 hotel rooms on a property that size. But $300 million is still $300 million. Our range was well below the asking price. We figured that if Tim and I each put up $20 million, and Andre and Perry put in another $10 million, we could borrow $175 million and make an offer on a property for roughly $225 million. Yeah, it's a great deal when you can get a $2,000 suit for $1,000. But it's not so great if you've got $600 in your pocket.

Tim's instincts urged him to hit the gas. He started working with numbers and finance guys to try to make it happen. His mind was back in the day when he could write a check to the *L.A. Times* advertising department on Wednesday with no money in his checking account because he felt in his gut he'd be able to come up with the cash by Monday morning.

It goes without saying that my instincts reached out for the brakes. My pain-in-the-ass questions kept forcing Tim's big ideas to the ground. That pissed him off. But I kept reminding him that when you've got nothing, you've got nothing to lose. When you've got $100 million, you've got $100 million to lose.

But after everything we'd been through, he was just counting on me—and my $20 million.

"What the fuck, Tom, just trust me!"

Of course I trusted him. I trusted him like a brother. But I wasn't the guy on the frozen lake anymore. I'd been cautiously negotiating with Barry Diller. I understood due diligence. It didn't matter how much I trusted Tim. A deal is a deal. I was going to understand every aspect of it. Until I did, I was going to plow through it with the same due diligence whether I was dealing with Tim, Barry Diller, or Phyllis Diller.

"Tom, are you looking for a way not to do the deal?" Tim would say. "Seriously, we're trying to get into this business. Keep your mind open."

"My mind is open. This is going to cost us $300 million and *then* we're going to have to renovate."

"They just redid the rooms."

"They *say* they redid the rooms. They redid the carpeting and some fixtures in *some* of the rooms. It'll cost another $100 million to do them all right. So now we're at $400 million. If we borrow to reach that number, we may not even be able to make our interest payments."

I'd inspected the place down to the boiler room. Tim kept insisting that I had lost sight of the big picture.

Our arguments kept bringing us back to our original game plan. We could comfortably offer $225 million. That's just what we did, and we were rejected. The rejection couldn't have been timed better.

Just as the "no" arrived from the Hilton, we got a "yes" from The Golden Nugget. Its owner, MGM Mirage Corp., was now interested in selling it to focus its energies on its larger properties, pay down debt, and buy back stock. It was perfect timing squared. The overall valuations of casinos in early 2003 had fallen to an unprecedented low due to the slow recovery from the aftershock of 9/11.

The only downside to The Nugget was its location. It was downtown. If you start at The Strip and drive toward downtown on Las Vegas Boulevard, one of the first things you start to notice is how the prices begin to sag all around you. The $350-a-night room at the Bellagio slowly gives way to a motel with a cactus on the marquee advertising rooms at $29 a night, which descends toward a $19 motel room further down the boulevard. By the time you reach downtown, signs are advertising fried Twinkies for 99 cents.

The mayor, Oscar Goodman, was constantly trying to figure out ways to revitalize downtown. Any man who can go from an attorney who represented mafia figures to the mayor of one of America's fastest-growing cities cannot be counted out. So there was a glimmer of optimism.

On the other hand, as the investor Warren Buffett has cautioned, turnarounds rarely turn around. Downtown Las Vegas certainly was a turnaround. The Golden Nugget wasn't, though. It was making $30 million a year. Tim went to check it out.

We'd been to The Nugget dozens of times to discuss rooms for Travelscape. But this was a different trip. Tim wanted to see if he could imagine owning it. He stood before the iconic arched entranceway flashing neon and stepped inside. There was a painting on the wall in the lobby—a portrait of the casino back when Steve Wynn first ran the place. The brilliant colors make it instantly recognizable as the work of LeRoy Neiman. But if you weren't tipped off, you might not notice the faces at the bottom left hand corner. There was Steve, Kenny Rogers—The Golden Nugget's director of entertainment at the time—and Frank Sinatra. The vibe coming off this painting was exactly what Tim wanted to bring back.

He stopped and recalled the great TV commercial back in the '80s that Wynn did with Sinatra, the one where Frank walks in and Steve heads over to greet him. "Hi, Mr. Sinatra," he says. "I'm Steve Wynn, and I own this place." Sinatra tucks some cash in Wynn's palm and says, "Make sure I have enough towels."

The thought of owning the same joint where he'd had the buffet breakfast as a kid after Sunday mass made Tim smile. But he had to make sure it felt right in the present.

He passed the sixty-one-pound golden nugget on display that we later found out was a fake, a replica of the real golden nugget that the MGM Mirage had locked away. But the phony was behind glass, and how the hell would anybody know the difference? It sure looked like history. The marble floors in the lobby were buffed. The crystal chandeliers were cleaned by hand. The joint was old, but it was old in the way the Waldorf-Astoria is old. You don't think of the Waldorf as old. You think of it as classic.

The MGM Mirage had put some effort into polishing The Nugget up. The casino floor was small, but that made every trip a short walk. Nobody would have to check in at the front desk, walk way past the casino to reach the elevator to go to the fiftieth floor, stop sixteen times on the way up, then walk a half mile down the hall to get to his or her room. On the way down, the elevators emptied right into the casino. You always felt like you were in the middle of the action. It was comfortable—a four-star hotel with two-star prices and a clientele that had been coming for years. There was a feel to The Nugget, impossible to describe or re-create, that let you know you were in a place like no other.

Tim walked over to a blackjack table and conspicuously pulled out a wad of cash. It was the first time in his life that he wanted to lose money. He wanted to see if a host would come over and offer him a free meal and a player's card, find out where he lived, maybe get a phone number to invite him back. A host did come over. He did ask Tim if he had a player's card. When Tim said no, that he was just messing around, the host left him alone. If we buy the joint, Tim thought, that might be the first guy fired.

Tim blew about three grand at the blackjack table and felt good when nobody approached him to comp his dinner. If a host had done everything that Tim thought he should've done, we might've felt that there was little to improve upon. But there was plenty. The Nugget was bringing in $30 million a year. Maybe we could get it up to $40 million.

Tim stepped outside, wandered through some of the other casinos, and then along Fremont Street. It was sad that a jewel like The Nugget was glittering across the street from a jail. But there were more people walking on Fremont Street than there were in front of Treasure Island on The Strip. They were much more likely to pass through the doors of The Nugget because The Nugget was the grand dame of downtown. People didn't come downtown to play at Fitzgerald's. If you were strolling downtown, sooner or later you'd wind up at The Nugget.

When I drove over with Tim not long afterward, I saw many of the same images. It was busy, not bustling. Polite, but not overly friendly. Good, but not great. It wasn't exactly a turnaround job, but there was a huge upside.

We were lucky that the MGM Mirage execs didn't want to sell to just anyone. They didn't want to see The Nugget in the hands of one of their corporate competitors. They liked the idea of handing it over to young guys with energy and fresh ideas.

We offered $190 million.

They asked for $225 million.

After several rounds of negotiations that got down to the real sixty-one-pound golden nugget that was locked away in a vault, we settled at $215 million. We still had to get financing and a gaming license. But if everything worked out, we'd get The Golden Nugget property downtown, a sister hotel-casino in Laughlin, and the real golden nugget that was locked away. We made the announcement and met the staff. It felt great when Bobby Baldwin, an MGM executive and a legend at The Nugget for decades, joined us to assure everyone working at the hotel that they were in good hands.

Not long afterward, we went to Andre's home to celebrate the completion of the first stage. It was one of those meals that you never forget. Andre's kids were running around, his son hitting a ball dangling from the ceiling with a baseball bat, while his wife, Steffi Graf, tried to keep up with them. Andre had a large barbecue fork in his hand. Steaks were marinating. Andre wouldn't let anybody see his marinade. It was top secret.

"How do you want your steaks?" he asked. "*Exactly* how?" We tried to go outside to see him working by the grill, but he said, "No, no, you guys stay inside."

When he put a steak down on my plate, he threw his hands up in the air and said, "Now, tell me that's not the best steak you've ever had!"

It *was* the best steak I'd ever tasted. Sure as hell beat the one I'd had in the first-class section of Northwest Airlines as a kid.

But the beauty of the moment was seeing how hard Andre was working at being a host. There were no chefs around. He was doing all the work, and nothing was beneath him. Tim and I had been talking for a long time about hosting, how we wanted to treat people once they entered The Golden Nugget—and the best model for what we wanted to do was right in front us.

We all paused for a moment around the table and said grace, thankful for the food and the friendship.

Some people might have suspected that we wanted Andre along for his name. Extra cachet, as they say in Vegas. They didn't understand. Andre has the chance to do dozens of deals, and he and Perry are very careful about the ones they select. Substance is everything to Andre and Perry—and it was one of the keys to our partnership.

The substance of our travel business enabled us to attract a seventy-year-old industry icon named Chuck Mathewson as an additional investor. It lured Mark Burnett and Fox to offer us the chance to star in our own reality TV show. When you're putting up a lot of your own money, when you've got folks like Andre Agassi and Perry Rogers on your team, you get trust in return. We crisscrossed the country to raise money for the deal and landed in Las Vegas ten days later with all we needed at an interest rate lower than we'd anticipated.

The power of substance became even more apparent when another of our investors, in for $2.5 million, got cold feet. As soon as Andre heard, he volunteered to go in for more money.

"You know what I'm gonna bet on every time?" Andre told Perry. "I'm gonna bet on us and the people who we grew up with."

"I'm with you," Perry said. "But there are a lot of other deals we're looking at."

"Don't worry about the money," Andre said. "Just make the bet. I know them. I trust them. And I'm throwing it down on them."

CHAPTER 8

WHO? ME? TOM CORLEONE?

Getting a gaming license in Nevada is a little different from getting a driver's license—and a lot more expensive.

In Nevada, you have to pay to be investigated no matter how long it takes or how much it costs. Back in 2003 it cost more than $100,000 for each of us to be investigated and pay our legal fees.

Even though you know you're being investigated, it's still a shock when State Gaming Control officials show up at your door and say, "Good morning. We're going to spend the day on your computer."

They go through your e-mails, your bank accounts, your phone records. By the time they're through, they know everything about you and the guy who washes your car.

Fair enough. It's their job to keep the industry clean. But the investigation turned into something out of a spy film one sunny day when my cell phone rang as I was driving with Perry.

"The FBI is in the office," my assistant said, "and they have some questions for you."

The *FBI?* About the only time I'd ever broken the law was when I rode an unauthorized motorbike down the streets of Barnsville in seventh grade. Even then I must've looked both ways about ten times as I approached each corner—making certain I didn't turn straight into a paddy wagon.

"Should we call our gaming lawyer?" I asked Perry.

"We've got nothing to hide," Perry said. "Tell 'em we'll go right now."

As we drove over, I couldn't help wondering if I'd done something wrong that I didn't even know about.

After a number of questions, the FBI agent came right out and put his cards on the table. "I know you're going to tell me the truth," he said. "Does Rick Rizzolo or any of his associates have a hidden piece of The Golden Nugget?"

That was it? I actually started laughing. I just couldn't help myself. The tension drained right out of me.

Rick Rizzolo was the owner of one of Vegas's strip clubs: Crazy Horse Too. The club had been around so long it was a Vegas institution. So was Rizzolo. He's one of the most sought-after gamblers in town. The Hard Rock kept a table on reserve for him twenty-four hours a day. Nobody else could play on it. Rizzolo often promoted charity causes, and he was a fixture at political fund-raisers. It would be hard for anybody who's anybody in Las Vegas not to have crossed paths with Rick Rizzolo at some point.

Besides, he's a very friendly guy and a lot of fun to be around. In the days after Tim and I sold Travelscape, we occasionally went to Rick's club to smoke a cigar and have a drink. There weren't even strippers soliciting lap dances in the VIP lounge where we drank. The VIP lounge was a place where celebrities could unwind without a hassle, and where friends of Rick's could get together. Sometimes we had dinner and gambled with Rick. But that was the extent of the relationship.

I'd been traveling to Europe frequently for Expedia so I saw a lot less of Rick than Tim did. But the FBI had been tapping Rizzolo's phone in an investigation dubbed "Operation G-Sting" that had lasted more than a decade. There were allegations that employees at Crazy Horse Too had beaten patrons with baseball bats and that customers were being forced to sign inflated credit card receipts. Our experiences at the club had always been friendly, and our only exposure to baseball bats or inflated bills came on the pages of the newspaper.

But suddenly, we were somehow being linked to the investigation like many others who'd walked into that VIP lounge—Robert De Niro, Joe Pesci, and George Clooney included. It's true, logs showed that I'd phoned Rizzolo eleven times. But anybody who listened to those calls could tell they were simply about the timing of dinner reservations.

"No way," I told the agent, "Rick Rizzolo is not involved in The Golden Nugget in any way, shape, or form."

Would Tim and I, asked a gaming agent present, come to Carson City to look at a few photos?

Next thing you know we're at the Gaming Control Board offices in the capital getting barraged with questions. Did we know this guy? This guy? This guy?

There were about four or five photographs of guys we'd seen before. One guy who worked for Rizzolo, it turned out, was the brother of a member of a Chicago crime family named Joey "the Clown" Lombardo. During the interview, a gaming agent said ominously, "We know about Naked Twister."

What the—?

One of the recordings the FBI must've picked up from Rick's

conversations had some mention of the game Naked Twister. It was mentioned over the phone as part of some joke. But I guess the FBI was casting it out like a fishing net to see what it might haul in. Okay, I've been to the Crazy Horse. I'd go as far as to say that when I was in my twenties and early thirties it was part of the young, single guy's circuit in Vegas. When friends came in from out of town, you took them to dinner, hit the Hard Rock to throw the dice, and then capped the night off at the Crazy Horse. It was a damn good time, I might add. But just because you have dinner at Piero's with the owner of a strip club and smoke a cigar in his joint, that doesn't mean you've been contorted on a Twister game board with the limbs of six naked women wrapped around you.

It was hard to tell if they were trying to build a case against Rick Rizzolo and the guys in the pictures, or if our knowledge of the people in the photos was going to be used against us when we stood before the state's Gaming Control Board.

We already knew that our appearance before the Gaming Control Board wasn't going to be a picnic. But now we quickly began to get the drift of two different cases that might be brought against us.

Here we have Mr. Tom Breitling, the bumpkin from Barnsville, who'd never even seen *The Godfather* when he went off to college. Who came to Las Vegas thinking that the VIG (the vigorish percentage) advertised atop taxis by casinos to attract gamblers to their baccarat tables stood for Very Important Gambler. Who thought the signs in front of hotels that said Valet Full *really meant* the valet was full, when everybody else in Las Vegas knew the sign meant you needed to grease the palm of the attendant in order to get your car parked. This is the same Mr. Breitling who was repeatedly outfoxed in the game of cribbage as a young man by his Grandma Johnson.

Could there be an easier mark in this city of 1.8 million for the mob?

And here we have Tim Poster. Could the Gaming Control Board members even begin to count the number of incidents in Mr. Poster's past that might raise an eyebrow?

There was that night as a very young man when he got cut off in his Lumina near the intersection of Flamingo and Las Vegas Boulevard, when he jumped out of his car and reached through the window of the offending vehicle with the intention of pulling the offending driver out, causing the offending driver's wife to race out the passenger door and start smashing the high heel of her shoe on the back of Tim's Lumina, distracting Tim enough to allow the offending driver to hit a switch and power the window up, causing Tim to grab the offending driver's hair as the window closed. The next thing Tim knew the offending driver's wife was back in the passenger seat, the offending driver was hitting the gas, and he, Tim Poster, was standing alone on Las Vegas Boulevard with a toupee in his hand.

Oh, yes, and what about that night Mr. Poster and his business partner enjoyed stogies and Sambuca at Morton's steak house? The night when a diner whom they passed on the way out said, "Thanks for ruining my dinner with your fucking cigars!" And Mr. Poster responded, "Excuse me, sir, but this is a cigar-friendly restaurant and we were simply enjoying ourselves—and maybe you should watch your mouth in front of the lady." To which the guy shot back: "Well, you should know you're a fucking asshole!" To which Tim grabbed the guy's coffee cup, splashed the beverage in the guy's lap, set the cup back down, straightened his jacket, and walked out. At which point the guy with the puddle of coffee in his lap picked up the cup and hurled it at Tim, who turned the corner just in time for the cup to sail by and smash into the forehead of a diner at the table just beyond, drawing blood and sending the poor guy to the hospital.

These were scenes that could've come straight out of a Martin Scorsese film. And I've got to admit, the images might well create a certain impression in the mind of somebody who didn't really know Tim.

When I first arrived in Vegas, we'd go to see Sinatra without a ticket, receive a hug from Nicky the maitre d', pass the legion of Frank's adoring fans, and get escorted to a seat at a front table. "How the hell did you do that?" I'd ask. And Tim would bend his nose with a finger to imply that we were "dialed in." It was a friend and two Benjamin Franklins that got us those seats—not any link to the mob. Favors are currency in Las Vegas. You get me in here, and I'll get you in there. To Tim, being a wise guy means figuring out the angles in order to get what you want. That's what makes a wise guy "wise."

But the Gaming Control Board had a very different definition of the word "wise." Even after our trip to Carson City, we had no idea what kind of grilling we were in for when we stepped into that first hearing. We should have known the moment we arrived. The toughest cases are always scheduled for early in the day. Ours was first on the docket.

To be fair, I should point out that it's a damn good thing Nevada's got a Gaming Control Board. The Strip was put on the map thanks to a man by the name of Bugsy Siegel, who opened the Flamingo in 1946 with $6 million of the mob's money. Even though Siegel was whacked with a hailstorm of bullets, one of which pierced his cheek, the legend of his murder inspired the shot-through-the-eyeball-while-getting-a-massage scene in *The Godfather*.

For years, the mob and the teamsters were rooted in the casino industry in Vegas. The Gaming Control Board is partly responsible for that no longer being the case. The cleansing of the casino industry, in fact, could be cited as one of the catalysts that drove the boom in Las Vegas. Every nickel is accounted for in the casino industry. It's exactly this sort of scrutiny that makes it easy for hotel-casinos to attract billions from Wall Street. It may seem strange, but Wall Street can trust a casino in Las Vegas a lot more than it can many other businesses because of the layers of accountability and the stringent monitors the state government has set in place.

On the other hand, the rigor of a Gaming Control Board investigation is said to have kept many high profile people from owning a hotel-casino. Nobody likes a trip to the proctologist unless it's absolutely necessary.

Owning a casino was Tim's dream. We wanted the license. The rubber glove was necessary.

Our first appointment was scheduled for 9:00 AM on January 7, 2004. After the initial pleasantries, one of the Gaming Control Board's three members, Bobby Siller, began to bring up a lot of the information that the FBI had asked us about—in a very ominous tone.

"Do you know a Mr. Rocky Lombardo?"

"Do you know a Mr. Vinny Faraci?"

We stated for the record that these were guys we might have eaten dinner with at a table of twenty. But whatever we said seemed to get twisted against us. Reasonable responses began to sound like admissions of guilt.

When the board members asked Tim if he'd ever loaned or taken money from Rick Rizzolo, Tim remembered a time that he had. His explanation was perfectly understandable. They were at a casino where Tim didn't have a credit line and Rick did. So Tim accepted a loan from Rick, and they hit the tables. This is commonplace among high rollers in Vegas. You could almost call it professional courtesy. Tim often lent money to people he trusted from his credit lines. But the back-and-forth triggered by the discussion of that one loan made it seem like Rick's hand was already in Tim's pocket.

Siller, one of the three members on the board, had a background in law enforcement, and he focused on the nights we'd spent at the Crazy Horse Too. He pointed out that the surveillance cameras at these clubs could also be used in ways that we might not anticipate—to capture moments that would prove embarrassing to patrons in the future. Such images, he added, are a red carpet to extortion.

He let everybody know that the results of the FBI's investigation of Rizzolo would be over shortly, and that some bad things were going to come out. "It's been my experience that you would definitely have been a mark," he told us—along with every media outlet in the state. "Something would have happened to both of you, make no mistake about that."

Siller's tone suggested we were doomed to wake up with a bloody horse head under our bed sheets any day now. It seemed absurd to us. But what could we do? Again and again, Tim admitted his bad judgment in continuing to speak with Rizzolo after our lawyer had advised him to cut off all communication. How could Tim make the world understand that he *had* backed away from Rizzolo? It just wasn't his way to completely ignore somebody he'd been friendly with, somebody who'd never done him any harm.

It was hard for anybody who didn't really know Tim to understand. Years earlier, while picking up business around town for LVRS, Tim would occasionally check into a hotel room, then check out less than an hour later. It was assumed by many that

Tim was using the room with a hooker. But in fact, Tim had paid the entire day's rate simply to make sure he had a clean restroom. But who'd believe that in Vegas?

Well, the worst was yet to come. Soon the name Jack Franzi came up. Tim's great uncle. Our beloved Uncle Jack.

"Mr. Poster, are you aware that Mr. Franzi is a denied applicant?"

"Yes, sir, I am."

"Are you aware that one of the concerns was his association with organized crime figures, illegal bookmakers?"

Suddenly, it sounded to Tim as if they were asking him to sever all ties with his uncle, the man who had helped put him through college, who was a father figure during a time when his own father wasn't there for him. As they looked at Tim, friends who'd come to the hearing were actually squirming in their seats.

Tim's restraint was being tested almost more than he could bear. The guy who once got into a fight over a parking space with a pediatrician suddenly had to stand at a podium and turn the other cheek as his uncle's reputation got slapped around.

In any other setting, Tim might have made the case that Las Vegas ought to be thanking people like his Uncle Jack and Bob Martin for helping to organize legal sports betting. But Tim knew that the slightest retaliation would be an alarm to the board and give the three members just the evidence they needed to deny the license. This was not a court of law where there are rights to protect the innocent. The board held all the power to judge our character. The three guys at the head of the room would make a decision on whether to recommend or deny us that license.

For two hours Tim remained on the grill. At one point the

board called me up to answer a few questions, and just when Tim thought he'd gotten off the hot seat, they summoned him for more.

When it was over, the three members of the Gaming Control Board didn't see fit to recommend that we receive a license unless the state could easily yank it away.

"There are too many questions here," said board member Scott Scherer. Without a limitation, he said, his vote would be no.

That basically meant the board would recommend to the Nevada Gaming Commission that we receive a license only if we'd start out on probation.

Probation? We hadn't done a damn thing wrong! But we were in quicksand, and our lawyer only pushed us deeper. "It's clear that the board wants a limitation," he said. "Hopefully it will be as short a limitation period as possible."

When the Gaming Control Board recommended a one-year limitation, we knew we were dead. What investor in his or her right mind would hand over money for a hotel-casino without knowing whether the owners would be allowed to run it for more than a year?

We were distraught as we stepped outside the courtroom only to find Mark Burnett's reality TV cameras waiting. We headed to the elevator and let the doors close on them.

What was there to say? It didn't matter, anyway. How can you have a show called *The Casino* without a casino?

The next morning, the newspaper was not a pretty sight.

Here we were, trying to do something good, and what we got in return was a public pummeling. The fact is we'd worked our asses off for years, and now a board member had dismissed our accomplishments as luck. Now, after Tim and I had spent a couple of years apart searching for and finally finding ourselves, the public was seeing a completely distorted image of us. All of a sudden, we were being dished up as either naïve fools or public enemy number one.

Once you've been painted like Joe Pesci in a mobster movie, it's hard to restore your image. People would never know Tim as he really was now. But I knew him. And the guy I knew was the owner of a successful company who went to the University of Nevada, Las Vegas to take an economics course just so he could get the final three credits for his degree at USC—even though the degree would have no impact on his livelihood. People would never know that, when USC refused to honor the UNLV credits after he passed that course, Tim flew to USC on Mondays, Wednesdays, and Fridays for an entire semester to take another economics course and earn his degree. People would never know that it was Tim who held me back when I first moved to Vegas and might have succumbed to her 24/7 delights. But that's a very different picture of Tim, not the sensational wise guy that had just been trotted out by the media. It's much easier—and certainly far more fun—to paint a mobster dressed in silk.

Phone calls flooded in from family and friends to lift our spirits. One unexpected call really stood out.

Only someone who'd gone through the same process could truly understand how Tim and I were feeling.

Elaine Wynn knew what it was like to be judged guilty before being proven innocent. The New Jersey Casino Control Commission had treated her and her husband, Steve, so suspiciously it wouldn't even let them attend the opening of their own hotel back in 1980.

"You're probably feeling it's us-against-them," she said.

"That's *exactly* how we feel," I told her.

"Don't," she said. "Don't underestimate the power of the process. And don't disrespect the dues you have to pay. This is not just about them riding roughshod over you. This is not about you being cavalier. This is about them getting your attention and saying, 'Listen, boys, you may be the next coming. But there are rules here that must be adhered to.'"

She wouldn't let us feel sorry for ourselves, and it was just the support we needed. In hindsight, I can now see she was saying, "Welcome to the club."

We were now living under a microscope, and we had to understand what that meant. We were asking to be the youngest casino owners in the state of Nevada. The state wanted to make sure that we weren't boys on a lark. It wanted to see us as responsible men.

In two weeks, we'd have to step onto the grill again when the Nevada Gaming Commission considered the Gaming Control Board's recommendation and made a final decision. The ante was raised. Our lawyer made plans to ask for an extension of the limitation. Every fact that had been revealed at the first meeting was sure to be scrutinized even further.

We'd gotten as far as we had by being ourselves, we decided, and that's the way we were going to stay. "It feels like I'm going to the electric chair," Tim said as he approached the hearing. Mark Burnett's cameras were there to catch it all.

It was painful to watch Tim stand up to yet another inquisition. It was painful not only for me and our friends, but for my mother, who was battling colon cancer, and my father, who'd already worked through his own misconceptions of Tim.

My dad is the straightest arrow in the world. There is simply nobody more trustworthy. For thirty-three years, thousands of people stepped into a gigantic metal tube and depended on him to lift all 873,000 pounds of it off the ground, navigate it through the clouds, and then land that tube safely six thousand miles away. Never once did he disappoint.

Now, Tim felt like shit as he looked over at my dad when my name was linked to the mob. And my dad, having gotten to know Tim, could barely keep himself from jumping out of his seat and giving the five members of the Nevada Gaming Commission an earful. "Let me tell you about these boys . . ."

By the end of the hearing, we were beginning to understand what it would take. The chairman of the commission, Peter Bernhard, asked, "So let me be clear on this, Mr. Poster. Am I right in the knowledge that there's not one member of your ownership group that has ever had any experience running a casino operation?" When we agreed to bring in a team of experienced people, the board began to understand the seriousness of our intentions. It extended our license to four years with probation. When the hearing was over, Mark Burnett's cameras captured our hugs. All we had to do was wait until midnight before we got the keys to The Golden Nugget.

As we prepared for the celebration at the hotel, an elderly man and his wife, who were parked on the fourth floor of The Nugget's garage, drove through a retaining wall, and their car plunged to the street. Both died. The man had hit the gas instead of the brake, and it certainly wasn't the hotel's fault. But we were besieged with news reporters as helicopters hovered overhead.

The enormity of our undertaking was right in front of us. Tim and I were now responsible for 1,907 rooms and suites, 40,000 square feet of casino space, and nearly 2,800 full- and part-time employees. It was like being in charge of a little kingdom. As the clock ticked toward midnight and we prepared to celebrate under these strange circumstances, our lawyers' cell phones were jangling at our table to sort out the accident while singing waiters were hitting operatic high notes.

Well, you can't call it an adventure if you know what's going to happen next.

At the stroke of midnight, January 23, 2004, it was all ours, and we lifted our glasses as Tim held up the keys to the joint.

"We've got the keys to the kingdom," Tim said.

"But you're open twenty-four hours a day," Perry said. "Why do you need keys?"

"To get in the cage," Tim said, "That's where all the cash is."

CHAPTER 9

STEVE'S BLESSING

Maybe the Gaming Control Board had good cause to wonder if we could be duped.

The first couple of days after we took over the casino were nuts. We were running around in a million directions without a moment to return congratulatory calls.

Lorenzo's brother, Frank, and The Sniffer phoned us again and again, but we were just overwhelmed. "Now that they're big shots," Frank said, as he and The Sniffer drove down the highway, "they can't be bothered with guys like us. I wonder if they're taking Steve Wynn's calls?"

A moment later, the phone rang in Tim's office.

"Hello, Mr. Poster, please."

"I'm afraid he's unavailable at the moment."

"Darling, this is Steve Wynn calling. Is there any way I can speak to Mr. Poster?"

The Sniffer was biting his lip. Frank was doing a flawless Steve Wynn impersonation on the car phone.

"I believe he's down the hall," Tim's secretary said. "Let me go find him."

A minute later, Tim grabbed the phone huffing and puffing.

"Hello. Hello. Mr. Wynn?"

"Timmy, my boy, how are you?"

"Oh, I'm great, Mr. Wynn."

"I just wanted to call and congratulate you on your purchase. You've got big balls, son. That's what I like about you. I just want to make sure you'll take good care of my baby."

"Don't worry, Mr. Wynn, I'm gonna take care of your baby."

At which point, The Sniffer and Frank just cracked up.

"I *knew* it was you, Frank!" Tim immediately shot back. "I knew it was you!"

Which only caused The Sniffer and Frank to laugh louder.

Which only caused Tim to slam down the phone.

Which only made The Sniffer and Frank laugh even harder.

To this day, The Sniffer claims, Tim will swear he knew who it was all along —even if you put bamboo shoots under his fingernails.

There were many things we learned when Steve Wynn joined us for dinner to celebrate our purchase of The Golden Nugget. One of them was that Steve would never say, "Timmy, my boy, take care of my baby!"

It was kind of surreal waiting for Steve Wynn to arrive as *our* guest. Steve was one of Tim's heroes when he was a kid. And I was still trying to adjust to the fact that I was now the owner of a hotel-casino. Even though four days had passed since we'd taken over, I'd find myself walking through the bakery and asking if it were okay to grab a cookie. "Mr. Breitling," one of the bakers responded. "You *own* that cookie."

As we waited for Steve's car to pull up, Tim begged me to get a grip. "Please," he said, "don't say anything stupid!" He never let me forget the day I thought the VIG meant Very Important Gambler.

But one of the things I realized after meeting Steve Wynn was that I truly belonged.

When you think of Steve Wynn, you think Las Vegas. But Steve wasn't from Las Vegas, either. He'd come from farther away than I did, Maryland, where he'd grown up working at his father's bingo parlor before going on to study literature at the University of Pennsylvania. Frank Sinatra was not from Vegas. He was from Hoboken, New Jersey. Dean Martin was from Steubenville, Ohio. Sammy Davis Jr. was from Harlem. The executive who helped Steve Wynn lift The Golden Nugget and build the Mirage and the Bellagio, Bobby Baldwin, came to town as a poker player from Oklahoma City. The man famous for running the Horseshoe across the street from The Nugget, Benny Binion, drove to Vegas with $2 million in the back seat of his car along the dusty route from Texas. Las Vegas has always been a magnet for anyone who wanted to take his life to a new place. It embraced anyone willing to take a risk and work relentlessly to make it better.

At The Nugget, I was once again following Tim's lead. He was overseeing the casino side of the operation. I was in charge of entertainment. Once more, I was green. The extent of my experience in the entertainment business was booking Kool & the Gang for our Travelscape Christmas party. I didn't do too bad, though. Anytime you can get Tim Poster boogying on the dance floor, you know you've hit a home run.

But this was a huge leap. It's hard enough to develop shows that cab drivers will casually mention to their passengers. In Vegas, you're competing for the same eyes that are staring at Paris Hilton in a million-dollar dress made of only gambling chips as she walks down a runway at the Palms. We had to do something dramatic to make people want to come over from The Strip. We had to take people back to the glory days and into the future at the same time. It was a tricky concept, and I wondered how Steve Wynn might go about pulling that off.

We greeted Steve and Elaine as their car pulled up, and we all headed inside the lobby. Steve stopped and stared at the LeRoy Neiman painting as if mesmerized by a song that took him way back. People who know him best say he's always looking forward. But for a moment, one of his fingertips rested on his lips, and you could sense the warmth of his memories bumping up against the passage of time.

The Golden Nugget was really the start of it all for Steve. Its success was his springboard. The Nugget had a history as a downtown grind joint in the days when a casino on Fremont Street meant sawdust floors and bets placed with silver dollars. There were no hotel rooms in The Nugget when Steve arrived in 1972. If you look at pictures from the '50s and '60s, you'd think downtown was a railroad stop. When somebody came up with the idea to put down carpet in a joint downtown, it was seen as a monumental upgrade. Imagine the odds against transforming a downtown grind joint into the very definition of the word "class."

That's what Steve Wynn did. The Golden Nugget was one of Nevada's first publicly traded gaming companies. After making a shrewd land deal, Steve used his profit to buy enough shares in The Nugget to get a seat on the board of directors in 1972. Those shares got him an office the size of a broom closet.

Within the next two board meetings, he catapulted himself out of that broom closet and into the role of chairman and CEO.

Once in charge, he added hundreds of rooms and built state-of-the-art suites. Then he brought Sinatra, Tony Bennett, Dean Martin, Willie Nelson, and Waylon Jennings to a stage that looked out upon 425 seats. The performances were intimate experiences, the type you never forget. Not only did the eyes of the city turn to The Nugget. People came from all over to stay and play there.

But The Nugget was not Steve's baby. Steve's mind is always moving on. I guess you could say that land is his canvas and hotels are his paint. Every piece of art he creates is different. Once a work is finished, his mind moves on to the next. After transforming The Golden Nugget, Steve turned his attention to Atlantic City for a while in the early '80s. Then he came up with an idea to build the most expensive resort in the world on The Strip—the Mirage.

People called him crazy. The cost of the Mirage was so exorbitant that it needed to take in a million dollars a day just to break even. And the people who called him crazy had no idea that upon completion, the Mirage had in its coffers only two weeks' worth of operating cash. But twenty thousand people lined Las Vegas Boulevard for the opening ceremony. And when the fifty-foot volcano out front erupted, all eyes were on the Mirage. It was tough to get a room afterward. Siegfried and Roy's tiger show became the hottest ticket in town.

After the Mirage came Treasure Island with its pirate ship and booming cannons out front that branded Vegas as the Disneyland for adults. A few years later he built the Bellagio. Nobody before had ever created a lake containing fountains that danced to music with the precision of synchronized swimmers. The equipment had not even been invented to give birth to such an idea. A prototype was laid out in a dirt field to see if it were even possible. A robotics company was then brought in to coordinate sound, light, and water. The fountains danced, and once again the city was wide-eyed. Inside the hotel, Steve had filled an art gallery with Van Goghs and Gauguins.

There was nowhere to take the "theme" form beyond the Bellagio. So Steve looked inside himself and lifted his art to a new level. After he sold The Nugget, the Mirage, Treasure Island, and the Bellagio to Kirk Kirkorian in 2000, he shifted his thinking. Rather than create a majestic theme that could be admired from afar, he built a mountain with a waterfall *within* the most lavish resort ever—the Wynn—and used it as a magnet to attract people off the street to an extraordinary gallery of cars, jewels, and great food.

The collection of Wynn's work over the last three decades has transformed a gambling town in the middle of the desert into one of America's fastest-growing cities. You really have to take a step back to appreciate not only the hotels he built, but their overall impact on Vegas. His hotels lured in millions of tourists, forced his competitors to keep up with the increase in visitors, and fueled the city's enormous expansion. There are medical centers in Las Vegas because of Steve Wynn. There are dental hygienists in the suburbs who have no idea that they live where they live and work where they work because of Steve Wynn.

It's said that owning a casino in Las Vegas makes you feel like royalty. That's just the feeling that Steve exuded as he entered the casino. Maybe it's charisma. Maybe it's mystique. But as Steve led us through the casino—pointing out changes made over the years and how the layout used to be—we couldn't help feeling like we were in *his* house. How could we think otherwise when employees who'd worked for him more than twenty years ago respectfully approached to say hello?

He stopped to point out a painting on the wall in a restaurant called Lillie Langtry's. It was a large portrait of a woman in the Old West—exactly the sort of work a casino restaurant commissions for $5,000 just so it can call itself Lillie Langtry's. But Steve explained that our restaurant was named after a real person—a famous lady in her day. Then he told us how he'd come upon the painting of Lillie Langtry.

The Golden Nugget now covers the length of a block on Fremont Street. But when Steve bought the hotel, it was only a third of the block. Over time he purchased one piece of property after the next to expand it to its current size. One of the places he bought and knocked down was an old dump called the Lucky Casino. Before he made the purchase, he took a tour of the place. Up in the attic he noticed a bunch of boxes and asked the owner what was inside them.

"Just a bunch of paintings collecting dust," the old guy said. Steve glanced at one and was intrigued. "If you want," the old guy said, "just take 'em."

Steve had the boxes sent to his office. There were about thirty paintings—all western motifs. He sent them out for an appraisal, and it turned out some of the paintings were fairly significant. This one painting of Lillie Langtry, he pointed out, was now worth about three or four hundred thousand dollars.

Tim and I looked at each other. We had $300,000 hanging on the wall and we didn't even know it!

That's Steve Wynn. A lot of us can recognize a Picasso or a Rembrandt. But Wynn sees jewels when others can't. The irony is Steve has retinitis pigmentosa—a disease that gradually narrows peripheral vision. Yet I've heard Michael Eisner say that Steve sees better than anybody he knows.

The beauty of having a dinner with Steve is that you think differently afterward. You hear a story about the painting of Lillie Langtry, and it makes you pay attention to your business or your property in a way that you just didn't two hours earlier.

We started our meal, and it wasn't long before Tim mentioned how much he loves Sinatra. Steve began regaling us with one story after the next. I won't even attempt to retell them. I'd never do them justice. But a moment of inspiration came when Steve told us about the time he asked Sinatra how he did it.

Steve loves the song "I've Got You Under My Skin." He'd studied every word of the liner notes on the album when it was first released and knew all the facts about the recording. But what he really wanted to know about was the process. "How do you do it, Frank?"

Frank's response will always stay with me. He started by reading the lyrics over and over to find the song within himself.

It was as basic and simple as finding trust in the ordering of a sandwich or the picking up of a phone. So basic that even a guy like me, whose singing is generally confined to the shower, could relate. The process that Frank used to create masterpieces was like the one I used to prepare a proposal for investors to raise money. It was about diligence—and finding the essence of something.

What do you want to say and how are you going to say it? That's where the creative process always starts. Afterward, you can bring in the great musicians and rehearse until you've got magic. But you're going nowhere until you've found your own voice. I realized I needed to respect that part of the process as I moved forward at The Nugget. I was going to have to read and reread the landscape around me. I needed to find my own voice.

For Tim, finding his voice was the easy part—for our song at The Nugget, anyway. He knew exactly how he wanted to run our casino. Maybe he didn't want to show up at every rehearsal. But his voice was natural, and it came from deep within.

He wanted to bring back what he loved about Las Vegas. He wanted to call back the days that he knew as a six-year-old, the days when a guy got treated like a big shot even if he was a small fry. That's what made Vegas special. He wanted to bring back the days when a guy from Buffalo would come for the weekend and later brag to his friends that he had a great weekend in Vegas—and it meant something. When that guy would return to Vegas—even if he wasn't a high roller—he would hear, "Mr. P., how you doing? We have a suite for you. You smoke Luckys right? You like VO, don't you? You're set for the eight o'clock show." Back in those days, the guy from Buffalo could lift a house phone and call anywhere in America. The call was on The House. Your money was no good unless you were gambling. Back in those days, you could have a conversation with the owner of the joint. You went home and could say that you knew him.

When you feel like a king, you don't feel bad about losing your money at the tables. Or, as Tim says, maybe you don't feel so good about it, but at least it puts a little salve on the wound.

It ate at Tim that corporations had taken over most of the casinos and made them so impersonal. It drove him crazy to see blue-haired ladies sticking their cards in the slot machines trying to get enough points for a free buffet. Don't even get him started on how the corporate casinos have ruined their own sports books and lost much of the action to offshore Internet operations.

Tim knew that if he treated people like kings and gave them the best gamble, they'd keep coming back. That was the history of Vegas, and he was connected to that history, so connected, he had an idea to replicate the very commercial that Steve Wynn and Frank Sinatra had done more than twenty years before.

At the time of our dinner, the Wynn was still under construction, so the timing was perfect. As Steve was "between hotels," he'd need a place a stay. The idea was to do a commercial where Steve came in the front door of The Nugget, and we'd greet him just as he'd greeted Sinatra. "Hi, Mr. Wynn. We're Tim and Tom, and we own this place." And Steve would tuck some cash in one of our palms and say, "Make sure I have enough towels."

Steve loved the idea. When he did the math, he realized that the age difference between him and Sinatra back when he filmed the original commercial was roughly the same difference between him and us now. The entire dinner took on the feel of Steve, the father, handing the kids the keys to the car. Make sure it's a joy ride, he told us. Downtown needed people who could hit the gas, people who could create energy and enthusiasm, people determined to think differently, people willing to make mistakes because you don't have successes unless you're learning from your failures. He reminded us how lucky we were. The Nugget had always been an intimate place, and we had the personalities to bring back the intimate atmosphere. You can't make somebody comfortable with money, he told us. Only a person can make a person feel comfortable. Your minds should never have to be boxed in by corporate bureaucracy. You don't have to wait for fifteen other sister properties to agree to execute a change. You can have a meeting and say, "Let's do it tonight!"

But Steve also told us where to slow down and maneuver carefully. We weren't on The Strip and wouldn't get much revenue from shopping. The casino was our core and—just as it was for him three decades before—this was our first experience at overseeing one.

Funny, there would be days ahead when the reality TV cameras would make Tim and me feel like prisoners in our own home. But now I'm glad that a camera was with us for a short time at dinner to record a story Steve told about the need for constant vigilance. A story that started with a phone call he'd received just after he'd taken over The Nugget:

I had been in the liquor business earlier in my career. The man on the phone was the owner of this bar over on Sahara Avenue. He had run into hard times years before — he and his wife.

All the liquor companies had put him on COD — wouldn't give him any credit. But we had decided to give him credit. He came out of it finally, and his place survived.

So the phone rings. It's this guy. "You remember me?"

I say, "Oh, yeah."

"Well, I've never forgotten how you helped my wife and I. I read in the papers you've got something to do with The Nugget."

"Sure do. I've got my lungs invested here."

"In that case, Mr. Wynn, you've got to come see me right away. My wife and I haven't opened up yet, but I have something very important to tell you."

So I jump in my car, drive over to Sahara Avenue, go into this bar, and he's waiting.

He says, "You see this back room here?" He points to a room that was all partitioned off. "Every night a bunch of your employees come over here. They have piles of chips, and they divide it among themselves."

"How much money you talking about?"

"Between $7,000 to $10,000 a night."

"Do you know any of their names?"

"Yes, I do."

"For example?"

First name out of his mouth is the casino manager on

*swing shift. The boss. The second name out of his mouth is
the assistant shift boss. The dice pit boss. The assistant dice
shift boss. Then the guy in charge of blackjack and about
nine dealers.*

*And if that's going on at swing shift, what about the
other shifts? Well I had three friends in the gambling business, and they weren't known at The Nugget. They came
down and for two weeks chronicled the wholesale stealing.
We had 350 employees, and I think we fired 195.*

The idea of firing more than 50 percent of the staff
stunned us.

"Oh, my God," was all I could say.

"We wouldn't be able to overcome that now," was all Tim
could add.

But Steve wasn't through yet.

*"My brother was going to Swarthmore College, and I
put him in charge of the parking lot. When you came inside
with your parking ticket, you could validate it, and you got
two hours of free parking.*

*Well, some people didn't bother to validate their tickets.
They just paid. We discovered that after the people left, the
valets would stand in front of the cage and punch all the
tickets on the machine until they equaled the entire cash of
the night. Then they took the extra cash out of the box and
turned in all the tickets as if they'd been free.*

*So my brother said to the guys, "Okay, no more stealing.
You've got to turn in the money when the customers pay."*

*And the guys who were working in the parking lot said,
"Just a minute. This isn't fair. If you don't let us take this*

money, we can't make it." They were so entrenched in the stealing that they challenged him.

The guy who'd been running the place was an honest fellow. But, I'll tell you something my father taught me as a kid: the minute you stop watching a person in gaming, money sticks in the hands of angels. If you're not diligent, you make thieves out of honest people.

Talk about lasting impressions. There was no need for video-tape. These stories were forever etched into our minds.

After awhile the executive chef brought a birthday cake to the table. We presented Steve with a full-page newspaper ad that his employees had taken out two decades earlier to wish him a happy birthday—neatly wrapped in a bow. But there was no gift that could come close to measuring up to what Steve and Elaine had given us. Elaine had been there with support when we needed it during the gaming hearings. And as we said goodbye and watched Steve head off, we definitely felt we had his blessing.

Our evening ended over drinks and cigars in Tim's office. Looking back, it might have been the first moment that we really had a chance to stop and reflect upon exactly where we were —in the office that Steve Wynn had once occupied.

The opening days had been a blur. Television crews lined up for interviews. Congratulations ringing off the hook. The slam of meetings. Boxes of documents to sign. Walking the floor and trying to meet all of our employees. I hadn't even gone home yet—and wouldn't for another week or so. I was grabbing a few hours of sleep every night at The Nugget.

Now that we had a quiet moment to sift through every detail of the dinner, we got a clear view of what was in front of us.

How would we attract everybody's eyes? And at the same time keep our eyes on everybody?

CHAPTER 10

THE BAIT IS TOO STRONG

People in the know were truly scared for us. If they didn't tell us at the time, they admitted it later.

To understand why, you need to know what it's like to look down on a casino from the eye-in-the-sky.

There's a huge perception that The House has every single player under constant surveillance. That the casino cameras will catch somebody the instant he steals a chip or counts cards.

That's simply not true. Thousands of people might be in motion simultaneously on a casino floor. But there are only a few sets of eyes scanning the monitors. The surveillance room couldn't possibly keep up.

The cameras are in place to verify suspicions—which means you need the right people on the floor to be suspicious. Robert De Niro sums it up pretty well as the guy in charge of the joint in the movie *Casino*.

In Vegas, everybody's gotta watch everybody else.

Since the players are looking to beat the casino, the dealers are watching the players.

The box men are watching the dealers.

The floormen are watching the box men.

The pit bosses are watching the floormen.

The shift bosses are watching the pit bosses.

The casino manager is watching the shift bosses.

I'm watching the casino manager.

And the eye in the sky is watching us all . . .

It's beautiful, watching De Niro gaze out upon the casino floor through the haze of his own cigarette smoke. In fact, if you asked Tim what it felt like to be in his casino at The Golden Nugget, he'll point you to that scene, twenty-one minutes and seven seconds into Martin Scorsese's film. But Tim had it better than De Niro. He wasn't acting out a few takes and going to a trailer. Tim was living his dream, 24/7. Not only that, but he upped the ante on Scorsese.

The way he was running our casino, *he* was gambling. In the beginning, even he didn't realize what could be lost.

His notion of how to run the joint came from a pure and simple place. He treated the players the way *he'd* like to be treated if he were the player. One of the first things he did was double the amount you could bet on craps.

When we took over The Nugget, the formula behind an initial bet was 3-4-5. That formula was the industry average. It meant that if you put down $1,000 on the pass line and your point became 4, you could bet up to three times your initial wager that you'd roll another 4 and win before you rolled a 7 and crapped out. If you did roll your 4, your payoff is 2-1, which meant a $3,000 wager would win $6,000. Plus, you take in $1,000 on your original bet. So rake in $7,000. That's what you'd collect up and down The Strip.

When Tim doubled the industry average from 3-4-5 to 6-8-10, you could bet $6,000 behind your initial $1,000 wager in that same situation, and if you rolled your 4 and made your point, you'd win $12,000, plus your initial $1,000 bet. That would give you $13,000. The exact same scenario would unfold if your point were 10. You could bump your $1,000 initial bet to $8,000 if the point was 5 or 9, or to $10,000, if your point was 6 or 8.

Like all bets, you've still got to win. But to big-time dice players, 6-8-10 was tasty chum. If you did make your point, you took in twice as much as you did at a corporate casino on The Strip.

The day Tim ramped up that formula, he knew every serious craps player in America would be getting a phone call. He knew that because of a trip he'd once taken to check out a riverboat casino in Tunica, Mississippi. Calling it a riverboat was a stretch. The river looked like a swamp, and the boat was no more than a floating warehouse. It was the worst casino Tim had ever seen. There were steel girders running across the floor. And there was nothing around for miles. Yet the riverboat was so crowded that people actually paid to get onboard and gamble. If you offer the best game around, Tim realized, the true players find you no matter where you are.

A million-dollar player might get flown in on a private jet to a 5,000-square-foot luxury suite on The Strip. He might be feted with $7,000 bottles of Chateau Petrus and be extended complimentary front-row seats to the best shows in town. But Tim was offering the best *game* in town. We were only twenty minutes from The Strip. We set The Golden Nugget logo on a custom gold Rolls Royce to add a little panache to the trip, picked up players on The Strip, and dropped them back off. At first, other casino execs thought we were crazy to try to lure in their huge players. Who the hell was going to bet millions near signs advertising 99 cent fried Twinkies? But soon that gold Rolls was gleaming all over The Strip. And it wasn't long before execs on The Strip were coming to The Nugget to see what the buzz was about—and gamble themselves.

Tim lured in the biggest players—the whales—by bringing in some of the best hosts. Steve Cyr had seventy players in his database who'd throw $100,000 on a craps table as casually as if paying for dinner—and fourteen who'd play up to $5 million. The swimming pool and tiki hut in Cyr's backyard were tips from his players. Richie Wilk was buddies with the cast of *The Sopranos*. Marsha Hartman was a screenplay waiting to be written—call it *Princess of Whales*. And Johnny D.? Our master of marketing. *Everybody* knew Johnny D. Michael Jordan knew Johnny D. Nicole Kidman knew Johnny D. When Wall Street guys couldn't get into a restaurant at home, they called Johnny D. out in Vegas to get them a table in New York!

It wasn't long before we had the buzz going. But that created a problem.

Tim thought that once we got the big-money players, the math would work itself out and the games would take care of themselves. Sure, smashing the corporate formulas would open us up to some volatile swings. But the rules of the games still stacked every deck of cards in our favor. There were just a couple of variables Tim hadn't factored in: the dealers—and the people watching them.

Think about it. Where does a dealer get started? Does he or she learn at a $1,000 table at the Bellagio?

No, a dealer starts out at a $2 table. At the $2 table, The House doesn't blow a gasket if a rookie makes a mistake. And where are the $2 tables? You won't find many at a hotel on The

Strip that has dancing water fountains on a man-made lake, that's for sure. Many of the $2 tables are downtown. Downtown was for grooming. Downtown was the minor leagues for The Strip.

The dealers work for tips, so naturally they don't want to hang around long at $2 tables. As they get more experience, they move from the $3 table at the El Cortez to the $25 table at The Golden Nugget. Long before we took over, there was a natural progression from The Nugget to the major leagues— Treasure Island, the Mirage, and, ultimately, the Bellagio.

Some of the dealers we inherited were inexperienced. Others had been around for a long time, which made you wonder why. Either way, inexperience and complacency are not what you want on the floor after you've rolled out the red carpet for every shark and whale in the country.

We didn't realize the effect the new clientele would have on our dealers, but it was like handing competent school bus drivers the keys to a Formula One race car. There were bound to be some crack-ups.

Even the keenest minds in the industry with billions in corporate backing and the sharpest dealers at their disposal could have problems in their casinos. Soon after the Bellagio opened, a player dobbed the deck with a dot of grease from his hair and used the marked cards to take the casino for $100,000. When this ruse at the blackjack table was discovered, management decided no longer to deal cards to players faced down. As long as every card was set on the table faced up, their thinking was, the players would have no need to even touch them.

Which was fine, except one particular blackjack pit was very close to the poker room. The poker players are the savviest card players around. They'd step outside of their own games for a break, stand behind the blackjack pit, and count the cards down. As soon as the deck was rich with cards favorable to the players, they'd jump in the game, make an easy score, and then walk away when the count turned or the cards were shuffled.

Poker players can track exactly which cards have been played. They understand the possibilities that exist with the cards in their hands and the cards remaining in the deck. And they understand the percentage of chance they're taking relative to what they've bet. They have to be that good. If they're not, they don't eat.

These are the sorts of minds we were inviting into our home. When you extend that kind of invitation, your people have to be as adept at catching the counters as the counters are at counting. Your dealers have to be as comfortable handling chips worth $100,000 as the players putting them on the table. The odds may be on your side when the game starts. But if your dealers are inexperienced, if they get nervous, if they screw up, then it's a different game—a game with odds tilted toward the players.

Later on, we could see how this problem flew by us. The Nugget was making $30 million a year when we took over. Its business plan was working well. The dealers on the floor looked professional. So there didn't appear to be a problem.

Plus, our minds were in a lot of other places. Tim was negotiating to bring Larry Flynt to The Nugget. Would The House give Larry $50,000 to make his first bet? How much of a discount would Larry get if he lost? And I was trying to bring Tony Bennett to our showroom. We were doing our best to meet every employee and greet as many customers as we could. Super Bowl madness was upon us the week after we took over. Then we were getting set for Valentine's Day. We were always running off to a meeting, talking with the press, feeding the reality TV cameras. There were so many demands on our time that our lives began to feel like a ball on a spinning roulette wheel. Only one night, when the wheel stopped, the ball happened to land next to the dealers at a private craps table.

It happened after Tim flew to Reno to have dinner with a million-dollar player in the hope of bringing him to The Nugget. The guy took a liking to Tim right away. Tim didn't even wait until the evening ended to extend an invitation. He invited the guy to hop on the jet with him and check out The Nugget while the night was still young. What the hell, the guy decided, let's go. Tim got on the phone during the plane ride and took care of all the particulars. He asked for a top-of-the-line suite, a private craps table, and our best dealers.

Craps is a tough game to keep up with. There are more than a hundred different bets that have different odds. If a player puts down $3,284 of chips and wins at 6-5, the dealer's got about four seconds to figure out the correct payoff. There are mental tricks that the dealers use to convert large numbers. They sure need them at a table where twenty people are going nuts at once. But that didn't seem to matter in the case of the guy who flew down from Reno. At a private table, he'd be rolling alone.

Well, the guy who flew down from Reno started firing bets all over the table. Problem was, the dealers couldn't keep up with him. They were getting confused and delaying the game while Tim stood behind them with his arms crossed—which had to make the dealers even more jittery and hesitant.

The guy who flew down from Reno was drinking. After a while, he started getting fidgety, and demanding the dice.

"Just pay him!" Tim hissed in a whisper. He was more concerned about not pissing off the guy who flew down from Reno than putting out the right payoffs. If we pissed the guy off, Tim was sure, we'd never get him back. If we made mistakes and overpaid him by $100,000, then at least we had a chance of taking it back the next time.

It was as if Tim's eyelids had been sprung open by a wake-up call that was two hours late. The casino manager got fired over that one and more. If Tim's eyes were opened by moments like that, you can imagine how the behind-the-curtain realities of running a casino struck me. You'd never think it from the outside looking in, but a single, innocent mistake by a dealer could cost a casino millions.

It's like the time one of our players came to the table with a million-dollar credit limit. He was having a rough go of it, and, after awhile, got down to his last $25,000 chip. With that single chip, he rallied, won all his money back, and then took a million of ours. Now, we didn't know if the dealer made a mistake in this particular case. But let's say the dealer *had* made an error. Let's say he made a payout that was more than it should've been while the player was spiraling down to that last chip. That one error would be responsible for placing that last chip in his hand. Without that last chip, the player never would've had a chance to win his money back—not to mention a million of ours.

You can be sure that if a dealer makes a mistake against the player, the player is going to catch it and ask for the correct amount. But if the dealer makes a mistake in the player's favor, how many times do you think the player's going to say a word? And these are just honest mistakes. What about when things get a little shady? One low-cut blouse can compromise a game. Let's say a woman with a nice set of melons sits at the blackjack table and draws a couple of 8s. She splits them right underneath her melons. The dealer pulls up a 7 and places it on top of the first 8. That gives her 15. Hit me again, she says, hoping for a card that will land her at—or keep her just under—21.

The dealer draws a 10, which bumps her over. But. . .

Instead of placing that 10 over the 8 and 7 and busting her, the dealer casually sets the 10 over the *other* 8. Now, she's got two hands in play—one of them with an 18. It looks legit in the surveillance room. Unless the guys watching the monitors are honed in on every move of that particular dealer, they'll never catch it. And who knows? Maybe they're staring at the melons, too.

Meanwhile, who's getting screwed? Not some billion-dollar corporation. The money is coming right out of Tim and Tom's pockets.

So the pit boss has to catch a play like that. Of course, the dealer will throw up his hands. "Oh, jeez, sorry, that was a mistake." *That's* when we can have surveillance hone in on the dealer. Or go back over the tapes to see how many times the dealer has made that same "mistake." If he's made it eighteen times in front of eighteen sets of melons, you know he's full of shit.

The owner has got to trust the dealers and the pit bosses to protect the integrity of the game. Most of our people did just that. But you don't know everyone's situation. Some have gambling problems. Some have drug problems. The dealers dress up nice and pitch the cards, but the truth is they may be vulnerable. When your inventory is cash, then *you* become vulnerable.

There's a story the bookmaker Bob Martin once told Tim that gets to the naked lure of Las Vegas. Bob had about $30,000 in cash stacked on his desk one day when he had to leave his home in a hurry. A cleaning lady was in the house. After he left, Bob realized that he'd left the money out in full view. "I'll bet," he said to himself, "she's gonna take it."

When Bob got back home, the money was gone. There was nobody else in the house and he'd only been out for a few hours. It had to have been the cleaning lady.

The next day, Bob confronted her. "Hey, I had a bunch of cash in here."

She immediately admitted to taking it.

And that's how Bob Martin let the story end.

"Wait a minute! Wait a minute!" Tim said. "Did you call the police? Did you fire her? What did you do?"

"I just told her to give me the money back."

"That's it?" Tim said. "You let her keep her job after she tried to steal 30 grand from you? You let her stay in your house?"

"Tim, listen, she *had* to take the money," Bob said. "The bait was too strong."

So you have to come to grips with those five words. You have to understand that honest people who'd never knock off a truckload of televisions or hold up a convenience store will be tempted to think that your cash is theirs when it's in their hands. You also have to understand that your employees will be watching how you respond after somebody has made a grab for it.

The first time it happened, our president brought it to us in the most professional manner. "We have a situation," Maurice Wooden said in the calmest voice.

Maurice loaded a videotape, and we watched a young guy in a baseball cap walk over to the cashier and turn in a winning slot machine ticket. The ticket valued $40. But the cashier took the ticket, counted out $3,000, gave it to the kid in the baseball cap and put the ticket aside. It wasn't a bright idea. The camera caught it all. Maurice had the details in no time. Mother and son. Mom was the cashier.

Tim is the kind of guy who—if the mother had come to him and explained that she had a problem and needed the money— might have given her a loan. He comes off as a tough guy. But the sign hanging in his office that read NO ACT OF KIND-NESS SHALL GO UNPUNISHED was really there to protect him from the goodness of his own heart.

Maybe if you're running a large corporation, you can be

detached. But he wasn't a corporation. He was a guy getting robbed. The videotape hit Tim in the belly like a mugger's baseball bat. Even worse, the robbery made him wonder if everyone who worked for us took the new guys for dupes.

"Arrest her!" Tim said. "Arrest her while she's working, and have her led out in handcuffs in full view of everyone in the casino!"

That wasn't necessary. The police were already on the case. Maurice later told us the woman had apologized. She'd asked if she could return the money. She'd asked if we could forget the whole thing. She was hoping for the kindness that Tim might have extended had she asked him for a loan.

There's a time for kindness. The only reason Steve Wynn had been able to learn about the stealing at The Nugget when he took over was because he'd been benevolent to that bar owner. But there are times when it's foolish to be kind. No, we told the women who'd stolen from us, no.

The next time a situation unfolded, it became less personal and more of a technical issue. You realize the bait is always large enough to make someone think they can grab it without the trap clamping down. So you need to study and adjust your traps.

But if you have to spend this much energy watching people on your team who simply can't help themselves, think of the precautions you need against people who come through your doors with the sole purpose of robbing you blind.

I'd listen in amazement to Pete Kaufman, who for years worked at the Barbary Coast and the Bellagio trying to catch the cheats, as he talked about the diligence the guys on the floor needed to flush out the teams of scam artists that constantly attacked the casinos.

Pete is the son of a cardiologist, and he approached his job with the intensity of a surgeon. Still, it took him hours to catch on to a player sitting at third base on a blackjack table who always seemed to make the correct play based on a card he wasn't supposed to know—the dealer's hole card. Even when this player lost a hand, he'd made exactly the right move based on the percentages.

A monitor in surveillance would barely register anything suspicious about the guy on third base. The camera was taking in the layout of the table, the cards, and the variation in bets. The only indicator that the guy on third base was cheating was his growing pile of chips. If you were looking at only the deck, his hand, and his chips—like the guys in surveillance—it would be almost impossible to sniff out his operation.

Pete smelled something wrong, though, from the casino floor and changed the deck. When that didn't work, he changed the dealer. That didn't make a difference, either. The guy's pile of chips just kept growing. So Pete kept studying the guy from afar. Finally, he noticed the guy on third base glance off in the direction of the bar. Then, after awhile, he saw a guy at the bar nodding. So he followed the head rotations of the guy at the bar. The guy at the bar was occasionally turning toward the slot machines. So Pete studied the slot machines. There was a guy playing one machine who didn't really seem to be focused on cherries and lemons. He was putting money into the machine. But what he really was doing was using his position to get a direct angle on the dealer's hole card from behind. Every time the dealer lifted his hole card to check if he had blackjack, the guy at the slot machines scoped it. As soon as he did, he signaled the hole card to the guy at the bar, who signaled it to the guy on third base.

Pete needed proof. So he got a long computer printout and positioned himself between the guy at the bar and the guy on third base. He opened the printout, spread it like the wings of a bird, and pretended to read. The printout was perfectly positioned to block the view. Then Pete waited to see what would happen. In no time at all, the guy at the bar changed seats to reestablish the connection.

As soon as he did, Pete walked over to the guy on third base.

"You can't play here anymore," he said.

"What are you talking about?"

"I'm going to give you ten seconds to get out of here," Pete said. "If you don't—"

Meanwhile, the guy at the slot machine was already running out the side door.

The casino can distribute pictures of these guys all over the country. It can rig up an electronics system to determine if the dealer's hole card gives The House blackjack—so there's no need for the dealer to lift that hole card until all the players have gone through their hands. But there's no end to the scam artists, and no end to the ways they can sting you.

It took hours of Pete's time to figure out the ruse. And how can you know that your guy on duty is going to be as smart and focused as Pete? Bottom line is, when you hear a story like that, it makes you realize you never truly know what's going on right under your nose.

It's hard to fight when you don't know what you're fighting against. But over time, the sheer force of Tim's strategy was overwhelming the problems that previously existed or that the strategy had created. So many more people were coming in to play that we had to hire more dealers. So much more money was on the tables that the volume of tips shot way up. The Internet sites used by dealers to track the average weekly tips by casino showed us climbing in the rankings. We began to attract experienced dealers from The Strip who wanted to get in on the action. One young woman working at our tables was making more than her mom—and her mom was dealing at the Mirage.

In a place where even the cameras couldn't tell you everything that was going on, we at least knew one thing: Money was pouring in.

Once, Tim watched a high roller go through half-a-million-dollar swings in minutes on a monitor in his office, knowing that one of our interest payments was due the next day. As the tension ramped up, he had to turn away. Tim and Steve Cyr left The Nugget and headed down the street to the Dairy Queen. It was exactly this sort of scenario that some of the smartest guys in Vegas anticipated. They thought we'd be overwhelmed and out of business in no time.

Tim called in twenty minutes later to see how the high roller was doing. He found out we'd made millions in about the time it took him to down a Peanut Buster Parfait.

CHAPTER 11

FLY ME TO THE MOON

There are moments that never go away, that become part of who you are, no matter where your life leads. One of those moments occurred for me about two months after we took over The Nugget, on March 5, 2004, when Tony Bennett walked into the joint. I remember the moment like it was yesterday—and I wish it were yesterday.

Although I had no idea what Tony was about to pass on to me, I immediately sensed that something was up because the world slowed down right in front of my eyes. Tony was wearing a gold sports coat, blue tie, and a pocket square, and he looked like I hope to look when I'm seventy-eight years old. There was a serenity coming off of him, and maybe it struck me all the more because I'd been working nonstop for two months with reality TV cameras trailing me sixteen hours a day. There were nights I was so exhausted I didn't even go home. I just flopped in a bed in one of our hotel rooms as one day tumbled into the next.

Just shaking Tony Bennett's hand and hearing him say hello made me smile. It's a piece of art, his voice. It's so pleasant that you can't help but stop and appreciate it when he orders tuna for lunch. Not long ago, Tony put out a CD of duets with some of the greatest musicians in the world. He performed his hits with Barbra Streisand, Paul McCartney, Celine Dion, Bono, K. D. Lang, Stevie Wonder, Sting, Elton John, James Taylor, and, I suppose I could list them all. But my point is of all the songs on the album, there was only one that wasn't a duet. When Tony Bennett recorded "I Left My Heart in San Francisco," he sang it alone. Was there anybody else in the world who could sing Tony Bennett's signature?

Nobody could've represented what we were trying to bring to The Nugget better than Tony. Our rebranding celebration was all about "Vintage Vegas." But there's also a quality of eternal youth in Tony that Tim and I wanted to bring to Fremont Street.

I've got to admit that I was proud of myself. Ten years earlier, I was driving into town with a hundred bucks in my pocket. Now, two months after we'd taken over The Nugget, I'd booked Tony Bennett for a weekend of performances and a gala to benefit Andre Agassi's foundation. Once again, it comes back to substance. It was Andre and Perry who'd made the connection. Tony is a big tennis fan, and he loves Andre's game the way the rest of the world loves Tony's voice.

Tony, Andre, Perry, Tim, and I had lunch like five old friends. Afterward, Tim and I walked Tony toward our empty showroom. It's an old room. Tony knew it well. He'd seen Frank Sinatra perform on the same stage decades before. You couldn't find a more intimate place to play in Vegas. There are only 425 seats. Nothing like it really exists in Vegas anymore, and nobody in the world understood that better than Tony.

That's because Tony had seen the city grow up. There wasn't a single tall building when he'd first arrived back in the '50s. Everything was ranch style back then. Louis Prima was the draw of the day in the Sahara's lounge. The movie stars were crazy to hear Louis scat, so they came from Hollywood. Frank Sinatra created the Rat Pack with Dean Martin and Sammy Davis Jr. as an after-hours lounge act to compete with Louie. Dinah Washington would come into town with two suitcases, say, "I'm here, boys," and sing until the sun came up. It was that kind of town. The owners of the hotels became friends with the performers. Early on in his career, when Tony wasn't drawing much of a crowd, he offered to return a portion of his salary to the owner of the hotel he was playing at. The owner refused to take it. The friendships are what Tony never forgot.

The success of Las Vegas lured in the corporations. They built big hotels with glitzy showrooms and created extravaganzas that attracted thousands—even millions when you added all the performances up. They put a precise value and ticket price on every seat and filled their registers. Which was great, except that when Tony arrived in Vegas to sing, he no longer knew who the boss was. It was impossible. Each joint had eleven bosses.

There were no small, intimate showrooms like ours left for a Tony Bennett. Maybe you'd find a few off the beaten path that could barely feed some unknown comics. But a theater with only 425 seats could no longer support a star night after night. We were able to make it work that weekend because we weren't worrying about tickets or prices. We wanted the world to look at us. And when it did, Tony Bennett is what we wanted the world to see.

Tony stepped up to our stage that afternoon and started walking around. It's not like he was studying the floor the way a golfer looks at a green before a tricky putt. But he was paying attention to it, almost like he was listening to it. Tim sat in a chair. I was standing next to him. Then all of a sudden Tony started to sing "Fly Me to the Moon"—a cappella. Slowly I felt myself sink to the steps beneath me, and I sat on the floor. The moment took me away, but it was so memorable I can tell you exactly what it felt like. Tony's dad used to climb to the top of a mountain when he was a young man in Italy and sing. It's said that everyone in the valley below would stop what they were doing, look up, and listen. When Tony sang a cappella that afternoon, I felt like one of those villagers.

Time had not only slowed down, it had gone backward.

Tony picked up a mike, and the band joined in. Over the weekend, there would be many standing ovations. But my favorite moments came in this impromptu rehearsal. How many people get a private performance from the guy that *Sinatra* called the best? It must've been how Steve Wynn felt being around Frank. What I loved most was watching Tony's diligence. There's a story that goes back to the days when Tony and Frank were in their prime, and they were booked to do a benefit at a hotel. The singers left their rooms and headed down to the showroom through the kitchen because that was the way many of the hotels had it set up years ago. The two of them were waiting in the wings to go on, when Frank turned to Tony and said, "How do you like that? Another kitchen." Well, this was another stage, just as that was another kitchen, but Tony was paying attention to every little detail, going over the sheet music with his band as if he were a kid preparing for his *first* performance.

Watching Tony, you couldn't help but pause and reflect. He would ultimately lead me to an understanding of how my partnership with Tim works. But at the time, I just sat there thinking about all the things that had to happen in Tony Bennett's life for him to be in our showroom at that very moment.

Tony likes to refer to himself as the original American Idol. When he first got married, they say there were two thousand women outside the church dressed in black in mock mourning. He recorded his classic, "I Left My Heart in San Francisco," in 1961. But not long afterward, the airwaves were filled with the Beatles, the Rolling Stones, Bob Dylan, Janis Joplin, Marvin Gaye, and war-protest songs. If the '60s represented a cultural revolution, then music was at its cutting edge. Tony's label didn't know quite how to respond to the changes. By 1969, Tony was pressured to do an album called *Tony Sings the Great Hits of Today*. The classy artist we all visualize in a tuxedo was suddenly repackaged on a psychedelic album cover. The experience made him feel lousy. But even worse, as time passed, it seemed the public no longer wanted to hear his music. By the end of the '70s, he had no recording contract, he got caught up in cocaine to dull the pain of his mother's death, and more money was going out than he was bringing in.

I'm not revealing any secrets here because Tony is open about this in his autobiography. One night, after his accountant called with news that the IRS was starting proceedings to take away his home, he overindulged, and passed out in the bathtub with the faucet on. His wife at the time suspected the water was running for too long, and when she went into the bathroom she found Tony unresponsive, pounded on his chest, and had him rushed to the hospital.

Tony came through a wiser man. Not long afterward, he called his sons for help.

Danny and Dae had grown up sitting on Duke Ellington's piano stool. They had many talents, but not their father's gift for performance. They started a country rock band in the '70s that you probably never heard of even though the name was quite distinctive—Quacky Duck and His Barnyard Friends. It didn't last long.

But Danny was good with numbers and understood how the industry worked. And Dae was a natural in the recording studio. Danny met with his dad's accountants. He structured a deal with the IRS to keep Tony's house. Then, as Tony's manager, he began to reinvent Tony's career.

Well, that's not the best way to put it. What he did was go to work on Tony's legacy. Tony stayed Tony. Danny just introduced Tony to young audiences through MTV, *Late Night with David Letterman*, *The Simpsons*, and college concerts. The kids, accustomed to punk, disco, and new wave, had never heard anything like him. They were just as mesmerized as their parents and grandparents had been.

By the mid-1980s, Tony was re-signed by Columbia Records. He could be seen at the MTV music awards and lifting up Grammys. Tony hadn't bridged the generation gap—it was said he'd demolished it. Danny had maintained Tony's musical integrity while boosting Tony's popularity. At age eighty, Tony's album of duets would be at the top of the charts along with the Dixie Chicks.

Demand for Tony's performance at The Nugget was overwhelming. I remember us cramming in as many extra seats as the room could handle. As the performance approached, I focused on certain areas of the hotel the way Tony had paid attention to our stage and the sheet music. I stepped into the kitchen and tasted the shellfish. I made sure the ice sculptures would go out for our VIP crowd at just the right time so they wouldn't melt. I wanted everything to be perfect for Tony. When I asked him what I could get for him, he had only one request: some bottled water.

The early years. My sixth birthday: a bike and a new brother on the same day.

The beginning of a partnership. Tim came to my graduation at the University of San Diego, May 1991.

Mom and Dad celebrate my dad's last flight as a Northwest Airlines pilot, 1999.

Tim, long before he discovered Brioni suits, with his bookmaking partner, Frank Toti Jr., and his Uncle Jimmy.

Their first meeting was tense, but Perry Rogers (*left*) and Andre Agassi have been smiling ever since. (*John C. Russell*)

Mr. In-credible, Richie Rich, and Naaygs celebrate the sale of Travelscape to Expedia for $105 million with Tim and me at Piero's.

The Golden Nugget has been the grande dame of downtown since 1946. (*Scott Duncan*)

Tim teaches "the square from Barnesville" a few tricks. (*Tomas Muscionico*)

Two artists: Tony Bennett with his son—and manager—Danny. (*Sony*)

James Gandolfini
with the real bosses

Steve and Elaine Wynn come
back to The Nugget to give us
their blessing and check on
their "baby."

There was nothing
better than watching Tim
in his glory. (*Scott Duncan*)

The one and only "Johnny D"

Tim, Andre, Tony, and I celebrate the re-branding of The Golden Nugget.

We jumped on a trampoline in 105-degree heat for this cover shot to promote *The Casino*, our reality show. (*Tomas Muscionico*)

Tim considers the portrait that Tony Bennett painted of us his most prized possession . . . even though it's hanging up in my house. (*Brittany Hanson BLR Life Photography, painting by Tony Bennett*)

Walking the red carpet at the premiere for *The Casino*. Anyone got a glass of Kool-Aid? (*Charles T. Lang/Driftwood Entertainment*)

The 50-foot heads: Our images were never the same after we appeared on the reality TV show and the world's largest television screen. (*Megan Edwards*)

The "eye in the sky" isn't much fun when you're losing $8 million. (*Scott Duncan*)

The Fertittas took Tim and me in like family. Frank Fertitta Jr. (*far right*) came to Las Vegas back in 1960 with $160 in his pocket and eventually started the Palace Station. His sons, Frank III (*next to him*) and Lorenzo (*far left*), grew the company, Station Casinos, into a multi-billion dollar empire.

Once the negotiations to sell The Nugget began, I refused to shave until the deal was signed. After Ed Borgato, our financial advisor and lead negotiator, slammed down his fist, we sold it for a $113-million profit.

The bride, Vanessa Tarazona, gets the official stamp of approval. (*Brittany Hanson BLR Life Photography*)

The journey continues. (*Scott Duncan*)

When Tony came out on our stage that Friday night and the crowd rose to its feet, the image that sticks with me is of Tim. I remember him looking over at his mom and Uncle Jack and swallowing hard. It was one of the proudest moments of his life. The kid who'd moved at age six to Las Vegas with a family that didn't have "two nickels to rub together" was now the owner of a casino featuring Tony Bennett. I'll never be able to describe how good it felt to help Tim have that moment.

The party never seemed to end that night. I must have started for home at about five o'clock in the morning. If I was tired, I didn't notice. Everything that transpired that day had given me a heightened sense of awareness. As I drove south on I-15 and left downtown, the color of the sky was what the locals call "Vegas blue." It's a very unique tone of blue—somewhere between baby and navy—that signals the end of the night and the coming of the morning. It doesn't show up every day. When it does, a lot of people don't notice it because they're just coming in after a long night, and they've had too much to drink or lost a lot of money and they're wiped out. Vegas blue is a reminder that the city is built on a beautiful desert. A lot of people think of Vegas as a façade. But until you've seen Vegas blue, you've never really seen the city. The moon was bright. I stared up at that moon and wondered how many times I'd driven home at three o'clock in the morning with Bally in the backseat and not even noticed?

One of the things about constantly striking out on new business ventures is you're always confronted with different situations. That means you're probably going to make mistakes. Believe me, you won't have to turn too many pages to find some. But there's a yang to that yin. When you push yourself into new worlds you're also putting yourself into a position to meet a Tony Bennett and a Danny Bennett.

The lessons I learned from Tony never stopped, and they always seemed to catch me off guard. One day over lunch, for instance, he called me an artist.

There are a lot of words you could use to describe me. But not once in my first thirty-four years had anyone ever called me an artist. Much less one of the great singers of our time—*and* a renowned painter! I remember painting an evergreen tree in first grade. One quick stroke down in brown for the trunk, followed by a few swift green lines across for branches. As soon as I finished, I bolted out the classroom door to play kickball. A very brief exhibit on Carol and Fred Breitling's refrigerator was as far as I ever got in the art world.

But Tony was serious. He brought up a conversation that he'd once had with Cary Grant in which they'd agreed that entrepreneurs were the artists of the future.

I never went to business school. Maybe if I had, I would've been familiar with the business-as-art metaphor. I've heard that when Steve Jobs was overseeing the invention of a Macintosh computer, he used to stare at the design of a Porsche in a parking lot for inspiration. Ed Borgato likes to compare Warren Buffett's holding company, Berkshire Hathaway, with a Jackson Pollock painting. A splash of Geico Insurance here. A splatter of Dairy Queen there. Throw in some Helzberg Diamonds. A little Fruit of the Loom. Dabble on the *Buffalo News* and Nebraska Furniture Mart. Add a big splash of United States Liability Insurance Group. If you look at the roughly fifty stock holdings in the portfolio from a distance as colors and shapes on a canvas you could easily see a masterpiece in profit. So, yes, Warren Buffett is an artist in his world as Steve Jobs is in his.

I could even see Tim as an artist. You definitely got that feeling when you walked into his office during the final years of Travelscape. It was dark except for pinpoint beams of light that came from the ceiling and focused on an array of computer screens lining his desk. The temperature in that room was fixed just above freezing. The Sniffer used to wear a coat when he went in to see Tim, and joke that it was so cold he could see the vapor of his own words when he spoke. There were people who worked for us who were actually scared to knock on Tim's door—as if afraid to disturb the thoughts of a temperamental writer in his garret. So you could make a case for Tim using a company as paper and pen to create his own drama.

But me? I couldn't see anything I did that compared even remotely to art. I viewed my job more as an extension of myself on the basketball court. I was the point guard who kept everyone involved. After all these years, I still felt like I was diving for loose balls as they headed out of bounds, and then slamming them off my opponent's kneecaps so our team could get an extra possession. Which, the way I looked at it, is all about smarts and hustle. So when Tony Bennett called me an artist, it really made me stop and wonder what the hell he was talking about.

It was through Tony's son that I came to understand. Danny had done more than revive his father's career. He'd given his dad the freedom to sing and paint whenever he wanted without ever having to worry about money again. He'd protected his father's integrity so that Tony could sing and paint with a clear conscience. He'd given an artist the time and the freedom to be an artist. When Tony talks about this gift, an expression of awe fills his face, as if his *son's* work is a work of art.

It's not that I reinvented Tim's life after we became partners. But there are moments when I can really relate to Danny. Of course, I never could have given Tim that moment at Tony's concert without all that he had given me. But that was the nature of our partnership. He had vision, and I had the ability to open doors, bring people and information inside, and help make his ideas a reality.

If things were reversed, if Danny were on stage and Tony were making the deals, we wouldn't be seeing either of them at the Grammys. My partnership with Tim would be a disaster if I were locked in a cold, dark room and left to miraculously turn numbers into huge ideas. Or if Tim had to remain in the center of a group of people and pay attention to details. Tim was the kind of guy who found himself in the middle of Las Vegas Boulevard with a woman smashing her high heels on his car and her husband's toupee in his hands. What better copilot was there for him than the son of a man who knew how keep an airplane level in turbulence?

Combined, Tim and I are definitely entrepreneurs in the best sense of the word. Our talents give people opportunities they might not otherwise have.

There are an infinite number of ways for an entrepreneur to impact someone's life. You could put out computer software, like Bill Gates, and make your product so important that people can no longer live without it. You could give people an incomparable moment by flying them into space—like Richard Branson. Or you could take over a hotel, create jobs, and put money in the pockets of employees who then have a chance to go after their own dreams. When you give someone an incomparable moment or a chance at a dream, that's when what you're doing borders on art.

If there were only *one* person at The Nugget that we were able to give that moment, it wouldn't have taken Tony Bennett long to recognize him. Tony is very conscious of how difficult it is for a young singer to find a place where he or she can learn the craft and get exposure. For the reality TV show, Tim and I brought a young singer into our lounge named Matt Dusk. Just

as Tony was the old master in a tuxedo who could be appreci-
ated by young crowds, Matt was the young singer in a tuxedo
who emulated the old masters.

Tony Bennett was one of Matt's idols and one of the reasons he wasn't back in Canada running his dad's box factory. So
when Tim and I told him we'd try to get Tony to come see him
sing in the lounge, he was overwhelmed.

All day long, Matt's band was teasing him about it, saying
they'd just heard that Tony was in a certain part of the hotel,
and then cackling as Matt ran off on a wild goose chase to go
meet him. On Saturday night, Matt went on stage and sang, but
Tony was running late. Matt went through his prepared numbers and, thinking Tony wasn't going to show, he got ready to
call it quits by singing "I Left My Heart in San Francisco." He
was in the middle of the song when he saw Tony come through
the door.

There was this comical "1-2-3" moment when Matt alerted
the band to switch in midsong to a new number. He just
couldn't bear to be caught stealing Tony's song in front of Tony.
It's a moment Matt still laughs about today. But Matt will also
be able to tell his grandkids about the moment Tony Bennett
applauded as he finished his show. That's a moment I think of
when you ask me what an entrepreneur can do.

Being an entrepreneur meant giving Matt the chance to
meet Tony Bennett. It's showing The Golden Nugget to six students I mentor at the Andre Agassi College Preparatory Academy and allowing them to see their lives as a canvas that can be
a work of art. It's giving every employee at the hotel the chance
to merge diligence and creativity in their jobs. What we did at
The Golden Nugget was unique. No corporation could have
created what we did in the same way. We'd wrapped the old
days into the new and made it personal. If we didn't have Dinah

Washington coming through the front doors with two suitcases and saying, "I'm here, boys," we had Tony Bennett's daughter playing in our lounge. Tony understood exactly what we were striving to do, because we'd brought back the day when the performer could be friends with the boss. We'd both given each other what we love about yesterday.

Over time, we became closer and closer with Tony. Which is why I felt like I could ask him if he'd do a little sketch of Tim and me.

Tony's artwork is amazing. If you looked at his painting *Monet's Gardens No. 2*, you might think it came off the brush from a famous nineteenth-century French impressionist. His watercolor of the Golden Gate Bridge moves you as much as "I Left My Heart in San Francisco" does. Tony's artwork is so good it hangs in galleries and museums around the world. But when Tim heard that I planned to ask him for a sketch, he was aghast.

"You can't do that, Tom! It's like asking somebody to borrow money. What if he says no? Everything is screwed up after that."

"I think he might *like* to do it," I said.

"Do you know what the odds are that he says no? Plus, you're gonna put him on the spot. You don't want him to say yes because he feels obligated."

"I'm not gonna put him on the spot."

"Tom, don't do it. It will be really embarrassing."

But as much as Tim hit the brakes, I just couldn't let him stop me. One night, the three of us were at dinner and I started to bring it up. Tim threw up his arms in a funny way and distanced himself from the table. "Tony," he said, "I got nothing to do with this!"

But I simply asked him.

"Sure!" Tony said.

"Reallyyyyyyyy?" Tim asked, and his voice got so high and squeaky at the end of that "really" you'd have thought it was coming from the squarest of squares from Barnsville.

"Yeah," Tony said, "send me some photos. I'd love to paint a portrait of you guys."

Some time passed. Then one day, the painting arrived. If my partnership with Tim was not a work of art before that day, it is now.

"My most prized possession," Tim will tell you, "even if it is in *Tom's* house . . ."

CHAPTER 12

FIFTY-FOOT HEADS

If your best buddy ever looks up, sees himself magnified into the size of King Kong on the largest screen in the world, turns to you in disbelief and says, "I never saw my head so big," you can be sure of one thing. Trouble is around the corner.

Maybe things were going too well. One day, Tim was dealing blackjack to the Sopranos, and the next I was being called up to the stage to perform a song with the Barenaked Ladies. We had not only captured the feel of Vintage Vegas with Tony Bennett, we'd also grabbed that elusive buzz that comes when cab drivers are talking about you, and everybody is wondering what you're going to do next. When a party that we were throwing got a mention in Norm Clarke's morning gossip column, we knew we'd be jamming that night.

Part of our plan to keep The Nugget on the lips of every cab driver was our reality TV show. There have been many other shows about casinos over the years. But most had been set up to mimic reality. We were opening our doors to something new. We were allowing the cameras access behind the scenes. Like everything else we did at The Nugget, we were making it personal.

From the moment we linked up with Mark Burnett, I figured all he had to do was point a camera at Tim, and the show would be a huge hit. When you've got your own Joe Pesci, how can you miss?

A few days before Tim, even met Burnett, he was talking on his cell phone as he drove into the valet at the Bellagio when he hit the gas instead of the brakes and rammed his Mercedes into another car. The airbag inflated and twisted his knee. When he showed up to meet Burnett a week later hobbling on a cane and explaining what had happened, the producer began to laugh. "Hey," Mark said, "save a little drama for the show!"

Perry was sure Tim would make a great television character—and that I'd compliment him well. But Tim didn't want to do it. He didn't like the idea of being followed around by cameras twenty-four hours a day. He was a private person to begin with—which is an understatement when you consider that I'd begun to call him Howard Hughes. He was concerned that he'd be portrayed as a compulsive workaholic and that I'd come off looking like a playboy. But most of all, Tim was against surrendering creative control.

I certainly didn't want to give it up, either. But if we were writing out a list of pros and cons about whether to do the show, the list of pros was far longer. Mark Burnett may have been born in London and served as a paratrooper in the British Army, but he'd certainly become a master at locating the pulse of mainstream America. *The Apprentice* was topping the ratings for NBC, and *Survivor* routinely attracted more than twenty million viewers for CBS. Burnett was offering us hundreds of thousands of dollars to put our brand before six to eight million people week after week for an entire summer. You couldn't buy advertising like that. To give you an idea just how much exposure that is, that's roughly *ten* times as many viewers as the MTV *Real World* show got when it set seven strangers in a luxury suite at the Palms Hotel a few years earlier. And *that* was a smash success.

Granted, it's not easy to make a television hit, and Burnett didn't have the lure of a competition in our show to keep viewers hooked like he did on *Survivor* and *The Apprentice*. But if he could work his magic, who knows, maybe our logo would start to pop up all over America like Donald Trump's "You're Fired!" hats. The timing seemed perfect. We'd be getting Burnett at his peak. Not only were *The Apprentice* and *Survivor* shining back in 2003, but Sylvester Stallone was working with Burnett on a boxing reality show called *The Contender* and Steven Spielberg was talking with him about another project that would come to be called *On the Lot*.

While Tim could see the potential in all of this, he never would've made this deal if he were on his own. This was one of those rare cases where he hit the brakes while I gunned the gas. I couldn't see it at the time, but I was already drinking the Kool-Aid. I'd gone to college to be the next Bob Costas, and though a reality show is much different than being a sportscaster, it was still television. TV had a powerful allure to me, and I didn't understand the world I was driving us toward. One of the disadvantages of always wanting to dive into new situations is you're constantly going to be naïve at first. I had no idea just how much Kool-Aid was waiting for me—or how much I had the capacity to drink.

Perry had been around. He wasn't drinking any Kool-Aid. To him, the show made sense on its business merits. So he put his foot on the gas pedal, too, and after awhile the deal just sped ahead. We all signed on with high hopes to do *The Casino* with Fox. But underneath, Tim wasn't putting his trust in the form or Burnett. He was trusting my instincts and Perry's judgment.

As soon as Burnett arrived in Vegas, he put us all at ease. We were truly impressed. When you get an inside look at the unique way he devises sets and thinks about character development, you quickly understand why he's a master at what he does. Burnett wouldn't have taken the show on if he didn't think it had the potential to be great. The only thing he really had to do was point the cameras at our reality.

There are plenty of casinos that invite celebrities in for publicity. But nowhere else would you find the owner of the joint on the floor dealing blackjack to the Sopranos. And, of course, Tim being Tim, he got us into hot water when he jokingly dealt only good cards. ("Oh, what's the matter? You don't like that one? How about this one?") We got fined for that little indiscretion. But even the gambling regulators understood that Tim was simply acting as if he were in his living room.

I guarantee you, nowhere in all of the concrete palaces lining The Strip would you find a happier casino owner than Tim. Or any owner using the master key to open the door on one of his sleeping customers at three in the morning, and then jumping on that customer's back. But that's just what Tim did with our pal Fritz.

When Tim noticed Fritz's girlfriend, Biata, wheeling a suitcase through the casino floor at almost three o'clock in the morning, he hustled over to find out what was wrong. Biata told him that Fritz had tossed down a few too many and gone to bed early while she'd stayed at the tables. When she arrived at the room, he was furious that she'd returned so late. "Only whores come in at this hour," Fritz fumed. Naturally, an argument ensued, and the next thing you know she'd packed her suitcase and was rolling it through the casino floor with tears streaming down her cheeks. Tim led her back up to the room, opened the door with the master key, and jumped on top of Fritz.

"You gotta make up with Biata!" he pleaded. "I will not have her crying in the middle of my casino at three in the morning!"

Fritz rubbed the fog out of his eyes, smiled, and the next thing you know he and Biata were hugging and kissing. When Mark Burnett said he envisioned our show as *The Love Boat* on steroids, I imagined this is what he was talking about.

You could develop a natural plot line just looking at the situations that Tim got us into when he opened up the limits. One time, Johnny D. called in about a whale from Europe who played roulette. Nobody in Vegas would give him the game he wanted. Johnny D. wanted to know if Tim would let the guy bet more than he could anywhere else in town.

The guy wasn't coming in on a line of credit. He'd be bringing millions straight to our cage. If he lost, we wouldn't have to wait thirty days for him to pay his marker, or worry whether he'd try to stiff us. We wouldn't have to negotiate a lower payment with him. The money was ours. All we had to do was let him put more money down at The Nugget than he was able to at any other roulette table in Vegas—and then beat him.

To Tim, it was like Fort Knox calling to get a game.

"Talk about a dream customer," he said. "There might not be ten guys like him in the world."

The guy was already in Vegas. We didn't have to send a plane for him. We didn't have to so much as offer him a suite. All we had to do was give him a roulette table and then allow him to bet his millions.

To Tim, the temptation was unbearable. Roulette, he knew,

is one of the worst games a player can play. It's not like black-jack where The House edge is only a small percentage. There's absolutely no skill involved. Of the countless bets you can make on a roulette table, none of them are very good—while a lot of them are *really* bad.

So you could almost hear the voice of Bob Martin echoing in Tim's ears.

"If you think you got the best of it . . ."

But . . .

The odds pay so well on some of those lousy bets, that if the guy put a mountain on the table and won, he could take us down in an avalanche. Take down the whole house! Tim. Me. Eugene the showroom manager. Ken the singing waiter. Drew the smiling bellman. Reinaldo the world's greatest window cleaner. Everyone.

But . . .

He'd have to be extraordinarily lucky to do that.

"We have so much the best of it," Tim said. "I can't *not* take him."

This bet was bigger than the money. Because—and I'll never be able to get this point across strongly enough—it's not about the money for Tim. Money is just a way that Tim keeps score of how well he handicaps life. This bet got to the core of why Tim wanted to own a joint in the first place.

Gigantic corporations with a wide range of hotels and billions of dollars in assets wouldn't give this roulette player the game he wanted. They wanted no part of this guy because they were no longer truly in the business of taking bets. That gnawed at Tim. He hated that most casino revenue in Vegas was now coming from the restaurants, shows, clubs, and shops. The 70 percent that did come from the casinos was dropped into slot machines—which Tim didn't consider gambling at all. It bothered Tim that every time the sun came up, Vegas was further away from the day when Benny Binion would give a rich guy with cancer a chance to plunk down everything he had on one last spree at the Horseshoe just before the poor bastard kicked the bucket. Or when Benny's son, Jack, allowed anyone to come into the Horseshoe and bet any amount he wished. Your only limit at the Horseshoe in the good old days was your first bet.

That was what Tim wanted to bring back. This roulette player was giving him a chance to be a Binion back in the day when it didn't get any better than being a Binion. So it came down to this. Would Tim take the bet that nobody else in Las Vegas would take?

The only request the roulette player made was that we didn't hock the game—that is, put nine pit bosses around the table.

"Yeah," Tim couldn't resist. "We'll do it."

The roulette player was a classy guy. He came in wearing a sports coat and tie on a Saturday afternoon. Talk about tension. For an hour, that roulette wheel was spinning at that table. It was just the guy in the sports coat, the dealers, and Tim. All you had to do was point cameras at Tim's face, the chips on the green felt, and the spinning roulette wheel. Tim couldn't smile or cringe or jerk his head to check bets on the table once a number was called. He had to act perfectly calm on the outside though anyone could tell that his stomach was doing somersaults.

After that hour, the guy in the sports coat turned to Tim and extended his hand. As they shook hands, the guy thanked Tim for the game. It didn't get any better than that moment for Tim. He'd taken the bet that nobody else in Vegas had the balls to take—and won a million bucks.

Now, you couldn't find suspense in a casino any more natural than what led up to and took place during that hour. The trouble was, that didn't appear on our reality show. Nor did Fritz and Biata. Nor did the Sopranos.

A little after 9:00 PM on June 14, 2004, our heads grew fifty feet tall, and reality was never the same.

Tim and I threw a red-carpet party at The Nugget on the evening *The Casino* made its debut. The festivities filled the entire hotel and spread out along Fremont Street under the giant canopy that has an underbelly lined with more than twelve million bulbs to make it the world's largest LED screen. This screen hovers about ninety feet overhead and is longer than four football fields. All the space under that canopy next to the hotel was packed with people. Downtrodden downtown suddenly looked like Times Square on New Year's Eve. Tim and I could barely move as we stepped into the crowd to introduce the show.

From the angle at which we stood, our bodies appeared contorted on the canopy screen. It was as if we were looking at ourselves in a fun-house mirror. When I think back on it now, that image couldn't have been more telling. Everything Tim and I were working toward was about to be twisted and distorted.

It's not just that the reviews turned out lousy, or that the governor of Nevada would ask us what the hell was going on. We were about to learn what could happen when you don't pay careful attention to a partnership.

There is a photo of Paul McCartney and John Lennon during the best of times that Perry Rogers keeps in his office. He keeps it there to remind himself: don't fuck it up. Whether a partnership is as creative as the one between the two Beatles during the good years, or as strong as the one between Perry and Andre, it needs to be constantly nourished. No matter how close two people are, no matter how much they achieve together, there's always the possibility of a wreck and a split. If that goes for the best of partnerships, you can imagine what might happen to a partnership that was no deeper than ink on paper. As soon after he'd put us at ease at the outset, Mark Burnett had disappeared.

We knew he had to shuttle between some far-flung island to shoot *Survivor* and New York to work with Donald Trump. So we understood. Occasionally, Tim and I would look at each other and say, "What happened to Burnett?" But we figured he was on top of things wherever he was. By the time we realized there was a problem, our heads had grown to fifty feet, and it was too late.

What happened, we heard later on, is that Burnett got hit with a low blow by Fox. He'd tried to sell his boxing show, *The Contender,* to Fox—but Fox was outbid by NBC. Not long after, Fox decided to start its own reality boxing show with Oscar De La Hoya and compete with his.

You can't blame Mark for being angry. But you can see exactly where this put us. We had a show on Fox being produced by a guy who was pissed off at Fox. We were caught in the middle of a conflict that we didn't even know about. All we knew was that we were without Mark Burnett. Looking back on it, we were his third-string show, and Burnett had left us with some first-time producers.

Everything proceeded as normal on the surface. There was a crew of about two hundred staying at the hotel and filming six days a week. But once Burnett vanished, everything changed. No amount of glue will hold together a partnership when one of the partners becomes a ghost. We weren't asking him to be there with a tissue every time we sneezed. But you can imagine how we felt when we heard that Burnett had come to town to meet with Sylvester Stallone and didn't even make time to say hello to us.

Even if he'd been around us for a little while during the filming, he would've sustained Tim's attention. But when he left, so did a part of Tim. Tim's focus went straight to the casino, not into *The Casino*.

This put the producers on site in a bind. They thought they had Joe Pesci. Now, they were scrambling to figure out ways somehow to fill a summer's worth of hour-long episodes—which put me in a bind. Suddenly, I felt like the point guard on a basketball team that couldn't do anything right. I'd expect Tim to be in place to slam home an alley-oop, and he'd be on the other side of the court. I'd look to pass to Mark Burnett and find out he wasn't even *on* the court. But there was plenty of Kool-Aid waiting for me on the bench whenever a time out was called. Life became, "Show up for a shot at eight. This is going to be great!" and "Your show is going to be Fox's biggest of the summer. You're probably going to be on Jay Leno." What a sucker I was. At eleven thirty at night, I'd find myself tuning into *The Tonight Show* to get a good look at Leno's set. Meanwhile, I didn't even realize that my younger brother, whom I usually talk to five times a day, was barely speaking to me because he felt so uncomfortable being around the cameras.

The ideas coming off Burnett's producers' clipboard didn't feel natural. But I embraced them. If the producers asked Tim and me to make a $5,000 bet on which one of us would win a race to work, I made sure we acted out the wager, hopped in our cars, hit the gas, and weaved through traffic like maniacs. The strangest part of the experience is there was no way to understand what was going on. With five thousand hours of tape being winnowed down into only sixteen hours of actual television time, it was impossible to intuit what the producers were really up to until the show was about to air. It was like playing a basketball game without knowing the score. You only find out at the final buzzer.

The days leading up to the debut were filled with interviews and press coverage. Tim and I would be on the roof of The Nugget jumping on a trampoline in 100-degree heat for a magazine cover photo shoot, and the photographer would be screaming, "Higher! Higher! Good! Now, can you guys hug each other? Good! Higher! Higher!" We'd come down sweating only to find more Kool-Aid waiting. There were flights to Los Angeles for walks along a red carpet to promote Fox's summer lineup. As the debut grew close, the Kool-Aid began to be served every half hour. *People* magazine at six o'clock. *Entertainment Tonight* at six thirty. *Access Hollywood* at seven. I chugged it all. When I saw my picture on the cover of *TV Guide*, I thought, "Y'know, maybe we do have a shot at Leno."

Then came the premiere. The show opened with the tension that Tim and I went through during the hearings for our gaming license. It was gripping and revealed the potential of what the show might be. But after the first commercial break, we immediately got a glimpse of where it was headed. A playboy named Big Chuck sauntered through our casino trying to seduce every woman he brushed up against until he ultimately convinced one to go up to his room. The scene ended with Big Chuck in disbelief after realizing that the woman he'd seduced was a transvestite.

Okay, kind of funny. But not exactly the brand recognition we were looking for. The show went downhill from there. Bachelor parties. Swingers. The wannabe cocktail waitress tempted to become a hooker. All of it casted. All of it staged. All of it obvious.

Look, they don't say "What happens in Vegas, stays in Vegas" for no reason. We understood that a good part of the lure of Vegas is sex, and we understood that sex would be a part of the show. But the sex in the show was fake and cheesy and it was smeared all over *our* reputation.

"When they bought The Golden Nugget, Tim Poster and

Tom Breitling vowed to return it to its former Vegas glory," wrote one columnist. "Great. I just never knew The Golden Nugget was a frat boy fantasy whorehouse in its previous incarnation." This columnist knew just where to stick the knife. *"The Casino* is so awful," he continued, "it will have you praying for, as Sinatra once said, 'a kick in the head.'"

The lower each episode sank, the more the producers reached for sex to keep it afloat. We'd filmed dinner with Steve Wynn, our meeting with the most charismatic mayor in America, and a poker game with legend Doyle Brunson. All of it ended up on the cutting room floor. That left plenty of time for the Trashy Lingerie Girls, bikini bowling babes, and a road trip taken by one of our youngest employees to a legal brothel.

Perry called Mark Burnett to find out what the hell was going on.

"Well, we thought we were getting Tim Poster," Burnett's producer argued.

"And we thought we were getting Mark Burnett!" Perry fired back.

I'd completely overlooked the underside of Burnett's success. I'd been so entranced by the idea of being on TV in front of millions, of being in the company of Donald Trump, Sylvester Stallone, and Steven Spielberg, that I hadn't given much thought as to how Burnett could possibly be in so many places at once. Tim and I were used to focusing on one company. If you shook hands with us, we were there to honor our end of the deal. Burnett was in a much different place. He could feel comfortable with a half-dozen shows on the air at once. Some would be hits. Others wouldn't work and be quickly canceled. That's just the way it goes in his world. He put his soul into the successes.

Tim will tell you that if he were doing it over again, he

would've thrown himself into the filming when Burnett disappeared. If Burnett didn't like where he was taking it, well, then that would have forced Mark to appear and work it out. Maybe the best solution would have been to turn the show into some kind of contest that allowed people to compete for a jackpot. Either way, we might have had a chance of creating a success.

But our partnership with Burnett degenerated into a summer of angry e-mails and phone calls. There was little that Tim and I could do about what appeared. We'd surrendered the right of creative control. You can imagine the guilt I felt watching Tim go berserk at the sight of letters from longtime customers who were aghast at scenes designed to make a fourteen-year-old boy chuckle. "If that's what goes on at your hotel," one woman summed it up, "you won't be seeing *my* husband again."

This was only just the beginning. We had a whole summer of episodes to endure. Tim closed the door to his office and retreated into a shell. The show created a rift between us. That was stressful enough. And I haven't even mentioned the wedge that fit right into the rift. The wedge arrived on the same night as the premiere party. The wedge was a Hollywood actress.

A tense summer of weekly reality shows was about to play out as Tim and I worked through one of mankind's oldest conflicts. What happens when a woman steps between two best friends?

CHAPTER 13

TWO PORTERHOUSES
AND A VEGETARIAN

Not that anything would have turned out differently, but in the hectic craze that led up to the night of the premiere party, I did something incredibly foolish. I neglected to give my date any guidelines at all about what to wear.

She arrived dressed in a mini skirt and a halter top—which couldn't have been further from the Vintage Vegas image that Tim and I were trying to brand. Tim's first glance at the Hollywood actress left him looking like he'd just bitten into a lemon. And I knew exactly what he was thinking. "What the hell, Tom! The cocktail waitresses have more clothing on than she does!"

To Tim, a woman dressed like that only made us look like playboys. And, well, it was hard to argue with him because Jaime Pressly *had* been on the cover of *Playboy*. Tim also knew that a Hollywood romance was exactly the sort of gossip that would find its way into Vegas Confidential, the column that everybody in the city wakes up to in the morning paper. There was no way a celebrity sighting was going to get by Norm Clarke. Sure enough, all three of us were in Vegas Confidential the next day. The event was mentioned. So was the debut of the reality show, as was the link between Jaime Pressly and me. After having transformed downtrodden downtown into Times Square on New Year's Eve, you can imagine how Tim felt when he saw the one picture in that column that represented The Nugget and the premiere party. It was a photo of the Hollywood actress who'd showed up dressed in a mini skirt and halter top.

"Tom," he said right off the bat, "this broad is not for you."

Tim Poster is one of the most honest guys you'll ever meet. He knew me well enough to complete my sentences. Our rottweiler shuttled between our homes as if she were our child. So Tim told me how he felt and figured that my relationship with Jaime Pressly would end sooner rather than later. In the meantime, what could he do?

That makes Tim one of the few men on earth who was not attracted to Jaime Pressly at first sight. Most people are, and the reasons go beyond the cover of *Playboy*. It's something that can better be explained through a story from her youth.

Jaime's mother was a dance instructor, and Jaime was about four years old when she did a Kermit the Frog routine in green leotards as part of a show before about three hundred people. Afterward, all the dancers had to take a bow by doing a forward roll or some other acrobatic stunt. Jaime's trick was to wrap her legs around her head and then walk around the stage on her hands. When the woman in charge said, "Okay, Jaime, put your legs down," the tights got stuck in her hairpiece and she couldn't unravel herself. So the woman in charge put her hand under Jaime's legs and lifted her up as if she were a basket. As the contorted four-year-old Jaime Pressly was being carried off the stage, she waved good-bye to the crowd—which sent every-body into hysterics.

That's Jaime. Wherever she goes, all eyes are upon her—and there will be laughter. Guaranteed, you'd laugh your ass off just sitting around with her, her brother, and the rest of her family while they're telling stories back home in North Carolina.

I met Jaime before she became an Emmy-winning actress on the TV show *My Name Is Earl*. Back in the beginning of 2004, she was doing a lot of independent films and looking for her big break. I was looking for a new act for our showroom. When Jaime left after our initial meeting, she knew that the act she was pitching wasn't a good fit for The Nugget. But I was also searching for a cover model for a photo book called *Vintage Vegas*. It was a collection of models dressed in the time period we were harkening back to at The Nugget. Jaime had been on the cover of *Playboy*, and she had a passion for vintage style and big band music. So I called to find out if she'd be interested. She was, and we made plans to meet at a Lakers' game.

I left The Nugget in the afternoon and flew to L.A. wearing the same suit I'd worn to work that morning. It was one of a bunch of suits Tim and I bought before the reality TV cameras started filming, selected specifically to convey an image as the owner of The Nugget. I felt perfectly comfortable in that suit. But there was Jaime at the Staples Center in jeans, drinking a beer, and wondering if I was showing up for a business meeting.

"Take your jacket off. Pleeeeeeease! You're at a Lakers' game. You look so uptight and stuffy. Roll your sleeves up!" She said it in a way that was comical, but there was a touch of embarrassment in her voice.

Courtside attire at a Lakers' game is casual and, thanks

to Perry and Shaquille O'Neal, we had front-row seats. The thing that you come to learn about stepping into a Hollywood romance is that you're always being watched and critiqued. You discover that the morning after you've been sighted on a date, when a local radio DJ and his partner come on the air and say something like, "Hey, who was that dork sitting next to Jaime Pressly at the Lakers' game last night?"

"Oh, yeaaaaah. That guy with his pants pulled up over his belly button."

Next morning, the radio talk show hosts were buzzing over who was sitting next to Jaime.

Look at the reality of who you are, Andre Agassi says, rather than the perception of who they assume you to be. I'm with him 100 percent. But it's a different world out there in L.A., and I was going to have to get used to it. From the very beginning, the cloth on our own backs seemed to be in the wrong place at the wrong time. I just couldn't see.

Part of *my* upbringing explains why I began to spend more and more time with her. Ever since my dad took me on those Northwest Airlines flights as a kid, I've wanted to head off to the unknown. Both my parents were constantly exposing me to new things in order to help me figure out what I wanted in life. Being around Jaime Pressly was like a trip to a new world—and that world was a whirlwind.

She was recording music, learning Wushu martial arts to prepare for a part in a movie, auditioning for TV shows, and starting a fashion company. I was now overseeing entertainment at The Nugget. Through Jaime, I was being exposed to this new world that I needed to know about. So I figured I could have it both ways. I could be on an adventure with Tim. And I could go out exploring with Jaime.

She certainly didn't mean to be a wedge between Tim and

me. Everybody wants to be liked by the best friend of the person they're dating. But there was no way she was ever going to fit in with Tim, nor in the group of people who'd been around me for more than a decade in Vegas. It was kind of like having a well-knit basketball team that brings in a free agent who's accustomed to getting the ball all the time and scoring thirty-five points a game. None of the other players could adjust. As the point guard, I figured that I could come up with a way to make it work. But even in the quietest moments at home, things were out of sync.

The phone calls that I'd usually get—"Hey, did you see the Barry Bonds home run?" or, "Hey, turn on Fox news"—stopped coming when Jaime was over. The more time I spent with her, the more the underlying tension began to bubble up in arguments over my schedule.

Normally, you work all week and then have free time on the weekends. But running a casino is not a normal job. Weekends are the busiest days of the week. So it wasn't fair to take off for L.A. to see Jaime and leave Tim when he most needed me. You can imagine his reaction when I made plans to go to L.A. for a weekend. In the cheeriest tone that Joe Pesci could possibly muster, he'd say, "Ohhhhhhhhh, that's okay, Tom. Go on and enjoy yourself. I'llllllll take care of everything here."

Asking to leave for even a few days was like breaking an unspoken agreement. Tim and I already had a girlfriend at the time, and her name was The Nugget. She took all of our time and our energy. We didn't have the luxury of making a mistake with her due to inattention. Just walking through every part of The Nugget took four hours out of a day—and both of us made the trip many times each week. Suddenly, I was going to leave town on Tim? After saddling him with the responsibility of being the star of a reality TV show? For six days a week during the three months of shooting, he'd put up with the cameras following him around when he didn't want any part of them. Now, the mere thought of leaving for a weekend seemed like an act of betrayal.

Jaime worked during the week. So if we were going to see each other, she had to come to Vegas on weekends. When she did, her attitude was: Tim, you had him all week. Now, it's my time. But there were all sorts of weekend obligations at The Nugget that ate up that time. After making the trip week after week, she started to get frustrated. "If you're not going to step back and have fun," she'd ask me, "why are you working so hard in the first place?"

To Tim, there *was* nothing more fun than living his dream on the floor of a casino. Even though it was an acquired dream for me, a part of me couldn't have agreed more. We really didn't know anything other than working that way. We thought anyone who questioned our work ethic, or who didn't see the fun in the ride, was crazy. Maybe Richard Branson had the right attitude when he said, "It's not work and it's not play. It's all living." I was still trying to figure it out. Maybe I still am. Finding the right balance is one of the great mysteries in anybody's life.

It didn't help that I had no idea how much time it takes to make a relationship work. Or that Tim had no patience for that learning curve—or for Jaime. Jaime claimed that one of the reasons that Tim didn't like her was that they were too alike, and therefore they were always bumping heads. Of course, Tim wants to bang his forehead into the wall when he hears that. But there's some truth in it. They both had powerful personalities. They're both self-made. And they both hate to lose.

While Tim started his business while he was in college, Jaime began even earlier. She moved out to California at the age of fourteen after her parents divorced, set out on her own as a model and an actress, and never looked back. There are few places in the world as competitive as Hollywood. If you can't make heads turn, you're nothing. Jaime Pressly fought for everything she got. No matter how successful she became, that sense of struggle never left her.

So it was only a matter of time before a tug of war started — and I was the rope.

Tim's real frustration wasn't with Jaime. It was with me. It was that I couldn't see reality staring me in the face. Jaime and I were a square peg and a round hole. When I couldn't grasp that truth, that's when he picked up his side of the rope.

The force behind Tim's grip can be described quite easily. In fact, it can be summed up by the time he went to dinner with a woman he was living with after she'd decided to become a vegetarian. As they sat down at the restaurant, she began an impassioned explanation of how unhealthy it is to eat meat, how it leads to the buildup of cholesterol, and ultimately to heart attacks and death. She went on and on, stressing how cruel it was to kill the animals, how wasteful the whole process was, and how everyone had an obligation to understand and change their eating habits. So, of course, when the waiter came to take their orders, Tim requested not one, but *two* porterhouses for himself. Then he asked the vegetarian to consider this. "Have you ever seen a sick-looking lion?"

You can see where this was headed. Or maybe you can't. As Tim carved into the prime piece of each porterhouse, the vegetarian went into a rage that culminated in her picking up his martini, hurling at it him, and storming off with the car keys. Tim shrugged, wiped off his jacket, and refocused his attention on the porterhouses. After dinner, he enjoyed a cigar and had a pleasant walk home.

Tim was always going to be Tim. Jaime was always going to be Jaime. Somehow I had to figure out a way to get the rope some slack when we were all in the same place. There was just no way it could work. I would've had to become somebody I'm not and leave the team I was with in order to build another team around her. Nearly everyone can identify with this. We've all seen cases when somebody new comes between two old friends. But there would've been much less conflict in this case if it had played out over a different time. The reality show had become like an oil spill that just kept spreading and gunking up everybody it touched—and tensions kept rising.

I'd asked a local entrepreneur, a friend of ours, named Billy Richardson to help us out on an episode that included the Trashy Lingerie Girls. The show identified him as the guy leading this bevy of half-naked babes into the casino—even though it wasn't Billy! Next thing Billy knew he was picking up the newspaper and seeing himself described as looking like a pimp by the same columnist who so enjoyed twisting the knife. Minutes later, his phone was ringing, and Billy was trying to calm down his wounded and furious mother who was all set to go for the columnist's scalp. Every day, it seemed, I was apologizing for something new. When I woke up in the morning and looked myself in the mirror, I stared straight into the face of a Kool-Aid hangover.

Even worse, there was no way to stop drinking the Kool-Aid. As bad as the show was, it did exactly what it was intended to do. It made us famous and brought thousands to The Nugget. It became hard to walk through the casino to get anything done because people were coming from around the country to meet us. *People* magazine was including Tim and me in its list of top fifty bachelors, and women were showing up and asking me to autograph their breasts. No matter how powerful you think television is it'll find a way to surprise you. I never would've signed on to do the show if I'd known that one of our youngest employees—the guy who'd gone to the brothel—would be filmed vomiting in a drunken stupor in front of the casino. But people traveled from all over to meet him and get *his* autograph. I began to wonder if the viewers who loved the show and wanted our autographs were really the people we wanted as guests.

Every week it got more and more surreal. But my mouth went dry when we got word that, based on the direction of the show, Tony Bennett would not take part in it. When I called the producers in outrage they said they didn't care, because they really didn't want Tony anyway!

This was over the borderline. You can imagine how I felt as I walked over to tell Tim. "Are you ready for this?" His hand went to his forehead and his lip curled in preparation for the worst. I don't even remember his response because I was in such a rage myself. The show was not only eclipsing our Vintage Vegas image. It was undermining our entire business strategy. If word got out that Tony and Danny wanted nothing to do with us, we were cooked.

My days were filled with phone calls to Perry, Danny Bennett, and the show's producers. "Look," Danny said, "you and Tim are what we want to be connected with—not the TV show." I had to convince him to stay on board. I had to get assurances from Burnett's people that Tony would be featured in an episode and treated with respect. In the process, Burnett agreed to send his crew back to Vegas to reshoot what was left of the show at no small expense. But you can't go back and reshoot reality—even when a lot of it has been concocted in the first place. Tim just couldn't put on the same shirt and suit and be seamlessly spliced back into a scene that happened months before—especially after losing ten pounds. Anyone looking carefully at the show could see that.

Finally, toward the end of August, the show's final episode mercifully came to an end. We'd planned a boys' vacation in Europe with some friends around that time—our first break after seven months of relentless work. I don't know what I was thinking when I asked Jaime to join us. Well, I do know what I was thinking. I thought that if I could just get Tim and Jaime together for an extended period where they could really get a chance to know each other, they might be able to blend. I was the point guard on the basketball court, remember, and bringing people together is what I do.

Jaime could see what was coming and asked me to reconsider. But I was stubborn and selfish. To Tim, I might as well have ruined his vacation before it even started. In fact, I did, though ironically the trip also brought about his favorite moment in the Jaime experience.

The details of the incident vary depending on who's telling the story. The disparity is small, though, only 1 percent. Everyone is in agreement on the other 99.

We flew off on vacation through Los Angeles. On the plane from Vegas to L.A., Tim claims that Jaime made a comment about how difficult it can be for her to go through LAX with all the paparazzi, autograph seekers, and fans that simply want to come over to wish her well. Great, he's thinking, I finally get a few days off, and I've got to take a trip with Elizabeth Taylor. The way he tells the story, he's rolling his eyes as she explains why she's going to put on a hat and sunglasses before we walk through LAX in the hope that she doesn't inconvenience the rest of us.

Jaime claims she never said anything like that to Tim. She says that under no circumstances would she ever say anything like that to Tim because she knew that Tim didn't like her, and she would never have given him that ammunition. She says she talked to me about it in private and wonders if I might have passed it on to Tim.

I certainly remember Jaime asking me to factor in extra time at airports when I traveled with her. Her upbringing in the South had ingrained in her a hospitality that made it impossible for her to refuse an autograph request. It's not like she was tackled by the masses as we approached our flights. Back then, she had a nice-sized MTV-generation audience. Point is, she was superpolite to anyone who approached her. I saw it play out over and again. It does take time to sign all those autographs. That said, I don't recall her mentioning the paparazzi and autograph seekers to Tim on the plane ride toward LAX. I'm not saying it didn't happen. I'm not saying it did. All I'm saying is that I didn't hear it.

Anyway, there's no doubt that Jaime put on her sunglasses and hat when the plane landed in an attempt to be inconspicuous. And there's no doubt as Tim puckered his lips, took a deep breath, and looked to the sky that he thought Jaime was trying to be conspicuously inconspicuous to *attract* attention.

As we went to retrieve our bags, several college-aged kids started running toward us. Tim's eyes started rolling. *Oh, geeeeez, here we go.*

Only they were racing toward Tim and me. They recognized us from the reality show and they wanted *our* autographs.

"Autographs?" Tim crowed. "Sure, guys! Absolutely! How about a picture?"

Then, one of the guys turned hopefully toward Jaime, handed her a camera, and asked her to take the shot.

As Tim put his arms around the guys and smiled, there is no denying that he was in his glory. If for some inexplicable reason Jaime couldn't see exactly how much Tim was savoring the moment, he made it linger.

"Let's get another one!"

About the only time Tim ever agreed with Jaime Pressly came after the guys had gone their way, when he turned to her and said, "You know, Jaime, I see what you mean about LAX."

There have been those who've theorized that Tim wanted to blow up the relationship by making the trip as lousy for Jaime and me as he felt himself. It certainly wasn't pleasant for Jaime, or for me. But it was my fault for putting us all in that situation. When you try to force something that isn't working, you're bound to make it rough on everybody.

I remember coming back to Vegas and pounding my fist on the steering wheel of my car, wondering why the hell nobody understood what I wanted. I simply couldn't fathom that *I* was the one who didn't understand. As Tim and I returned to The Nugget, the tension between us looked for every possible outlet, and the slightest mistake or miscommunication set off an argument. After he was convinced by poker champion Johnny Chan to purchase Snow Lotus Blossom tea gifts for our Asian customers, I was dumbfounded to discover that at $180 apiece the bill came to $60,000. The fifty thousand rubber bands with The Golden Nugget logo he'd ordered as money holders weren't nearly as expensive. But when you're not communicating properly, an unforeseen item like that can make you shout, "What the hell?" Soon you're screaming about something that you would have laughed over in another time.

Which is why Perry Rogers keeps that photo of Paul McCartney and John Lennon in his office to remind him: Don't fuck it up. Pay constant attention to your partnership. Snow Lotus Blossoms and rubber bands may not seem like much, but you never know what might begin to make everything unravel.

It would be another seven months before Tim was really at the end of his rope, and we had a blowup on our next vacation when we went to see Andre play tennis in Dubai. Andre stepped between us and explained everything he'd learned from his marriage and divorce with the actress Brooke Shields. He told me about the allure and façade of Hollywood, the misunderstandings and the pain, and how it led him to become a stronger person and find Steffi Graf. Well, you can't see what's right for you until you understand what isn't. I stopped arguing with Tim after my conversation with Andre. I was seeing reality.

Jaime was too. She was tired of trying to battle against Tim and force a relationship with someone who was stubborn and selfish, much too different, and would barely come to visit her. We were finally able to unlock horns and go on our way to find what was best for each of us.

One night I couldn't sleep and wandered out on my balcony overlooking The Strip as Vegas blue announced the end of one day and the beginning of another. I sat there wondering if I could possibly be lucky enough to find a woman who I loved and who loved me and who could balance a life with my best friend and my work. Lorenzo and Frank had each found that woman and that balance. Such a woman seemed a long way off as that night turned to morning. What I didn't realize was that my best friend would let me know when I found her.

Only now can I see how right Andre was. Everything that happened during that time was leading me straight to the woman who'd become the love of my life. Just as everything that happened in her life was leading her to me.

But the breakup with Jaime didn't happen until after Dubai, and Dubai was still a long way off when Tim and I returned home from that trip to Europe. The tension was ever present and mounting, and the distance between us was greater than at any time since the day we'd met.

Which meant it was certainly not the best of times for a guy to come into our casino and start beating the shit out of Tim and me for more than $8 million.

CHAPTER 14

THE GAMBLER

There were insiders who called Mr. Royalty's $25 million roll over the course of a year the most amazing they'd ever seen. It even surpassed The Run, the legendary winning streak notched by a Greek immigrant named Archie Karas. Archie pulled into town in 1992 with $50, got a loan from a friend, beat fifteen of the world's greatest poker players, then used a craps table at Binion's Horseshoe to multiply his take to more than $20 million.

Like Archie's run, Mr. Royalty's played out over time. It took a while before I got a grip on exactly what was happening. I wasn't sitting ringside the first couple of times Mr. Royalty came through the lobby bobbing and weaving as if he were entering the ring for a heavyweight championship fight. Sometimes Mr. Royalty arrived after midnight when I wasn't around. So I didn't even see him as a man. I first noticed him as a parenthesis on the Daily Operating Report.

Every morning a copy of the DOR would be e-mailed to my computer. The DOR would list in neat columns every department in the hotel, show a financial accounting for how it had done the day before, how that day measured up to the same day a year earlier, how we were doing up to that point in the month, and how that figure compared to its corresponding number the year before. It told me how many rooms we'd booked, how our restaurants did, how many tickets were sold at the showroom, how much cash flowed through our sports book, and just about anything else that had happened under our roof during the last twenty-four hours so long as it could be crunched into a number.

The DOR was generally very good news during early fall of 2004. In nearly every area, it showed consistent growth. In some areas, phenomenal improvement. Ed Borgato once looked at a chart showing our sports book revenues up 1,300 percent and thought the figure was a typo. It wasn't. It was Tim's open-up-the-limits strategy at work.

But I could also see in every DOR the emotional distance between Tim and me. After the tension of the European trip, we both burrowed into our work. Our jobs were the only place where we could escape from our frustrations with each other. We both tried to work out our differences by working harder. Even though we remained at an emotional distance, our work came together and the hotel blossomed.

Our rooms were booked, and our restaurants were filled. We found a dynamite nightclub act in impressionist Gordie Brown. We'd learned our lesson from the reality TV show and kept our television presence focused on our core customer with the poker challenge on NBC and a deal for the World Series of Blackjack on the Game Show Network. The future couldn't have been brighter. Tony Bennett was coming back. Country singer Randy

Travis signed on to perform when the rodeo was in town. Julio Iglesias put us on his calendar. We started looking into buying adjacent property and drawing up expansion plans.

All this positive energy burst off the DOR—with the exception of one line halfway down the page on the left-hand column. That's where I noticed a parenthesis. A parenthesis meant that the corresponding department had lost money the night before. Seeing $500,000 in parenthesis halfway down the page meant that a half-million bucks had been lost on table games.

"Oh, man," I'd say to myself. "We took a hit last night."

I started noticing this parenthesis halfway down the page more and more often. You can only say "we took a hit last night" for so long. After the fourth or fifth time, you say, "What the fuck?"

Gaming was the last place I was going to challenge Tim's expertise. But finally I brought it up.

"I know, I know," he nodded. "Listen, the worm's gonna turn." It was one of his favorite expressions. *The worm's gonna turn.*

But the more these parentheses kept appearing, the more I began to notice a change on the faces of our senior management team. I was wiser now than I was back in the days of Travelscape. When I saw the tightness in their lips, I remembered what had happened to Mr. Incredible's hello when he felt uncomfortable about our impending deal with Barry Diller. When Edward Muncey's response to "How you doin', Edward?" changed from "*In*-credible!" to "Okay," something was very wrong.

Our senior execs had been accustomed to working at MGM Mirage, where the odds were tightly coiled with very low risk to The House. They weren't used to seeing that parenthesis, and it bothered them big time.

"Make 'em eat like birds and shit like elephants," has always been the motto for running a successful casino. Much of our management team had never seen such volatile swings. They began to freak out when a few lucky players trampled the joint like elephants and didn't shit at all. After a while you could almost sense the execs whispering behind closed doors. When one of them pulled me aside and asked about our recurring losses at the tables, there was only one way I knew how to respond.

"Don't worry," I said. "The worm's gonna turn."

But Mr. Royalty was only heating up. And we weren't attracting enough big players who were losing enough to offset the damage Mr. Royalty was inflicting. If there'd been a lot of million-dollar players on the floor every time Mr. Royalty swaggered in, he wouldn't have mattered that much. The math would have taken care of itself. But one guy going for a knockout on every bet he made left you exposed to the unexpected when he got hot. Who could predict how far his luck might go? Just like in boxing, the punch that knocks you out is the one you don't see coming.

Soon everyone was aware when Mr. Royalty came through the lobby bobbing and weaving for another title fight, and then exiting with sacks of our money as if the championship belt were around his waist.

"You know what we're doing here?" asked an exasperated senior exec. "*We* are actually gambling!"

One day, after Mr. Royalty had walked off with another half million, I confronted Tim.

"Maybe we should stop taking his action," I said. "This just doesn't make sense. How could this happen?"

"The worm's gonna turn, Tom."

"Tim, he's beaten us for $4 million. That's half of our third-quarter profit."

"Trust me, Tom. The worm *always* turns."

"Look, everything else is going great. Every room was booked last night. There was a wait at every one of our restaurants. You know what they're saying about Gordie Brown? When you walk out of our showroom, your cheekbones are sore from laughter. We put all this together and then we pick up the DOR in the morning and find out we've *lost* money? What if he keeps coming and wins $25 million? It just doesn't make sense. No matter how hard everybody works, no matter how successful we are, are we really gonna give this guy a chance to take us down?"

Tim paused, but not for long. "So let me get this straight, Tom. Are you telling me that the laws of probability don't exist at The Golden Nugget?"

I saw a number in the parenthesis. Tim had different calculations running through his head.

"Look, Tom, the numbers say he'll lose. You know that like you know your name. He *will* lose. The numbers guarantee it. If he keeps playing, he *will* ultimately lose. He might *win more* before he loses. And he might lose it somewhere else. But for sure, if he keeps playing, he will lose. Do you want him to lose in *our* joint so we can get our money back? Or do you want him to lose the money he's already taken from us in *somebody else's* joint?"

What sounded safe to me—let's back off—sounded painfully risky to Tim. If we didn't give Mr. Royalty the limits and the game he wanted, he might not come back. Then we could never get our money back—not to mention Mr. Royalty's. That was the worst scenario for Tim. That made us a loser when we'd had the best of it. Tim wasn't an upper management guy. Every decision in his life was made so that he would never be an upper management guy. He was a gambler. The marrow running through his bones told Tim to stay in the game.

To Tim, it all boiled down to guts. And everything that would subsequently happen between him and Mr. Royalty can be traced back to that word. Guts. There's a story from Tim's childhood that helps explain it all, a story about a card game that took place nearly twenty years before Mr. Royalty walked through our doors. The name of that card game is Guts. It's a long story because it takes some time to describe the rules of the game. So bear with me. You'll see how it all comes together down the road.

Guts is like poker. Only it's played with two cards. A lot of kids in high school were scared of playing cards with Tim because of his reputation as a hustler. Guts was a good way for Tim to entice people into a game. Since the ante was only a quarter, the other kids felt comfortable when they heard Tim say, "Hey, it's only a 25 cent game."

While it was true that the ante remained 25 cents no matter how many times the cards were dealt, once you had a seat at the table, it didn't take long to see that you could win or lose big money.

Here's how. Everybody starts a game of Guts by throwing a quarter into the pot. Each player is dealt two cards faced down. The dealer also deals a dummy hand and sets those two cards in the center of the table. The worst hand anyone could possibly have is a 2 and a 3. The best hand is a pair of aces. To give you a gauge of risk, a pair of 2s gives you a reasonably good shot at winning.

Everybody looks at their cards and has to make a choice. Either you're in or you're out. If you're out, you've lost your quarter and you wait for the next game. If you're in, the game moves clockwise like a game of poker.

First, the remaining players try to beat each other. But the winner among the players doesn't automatically collect the pot. The person with the winning hand then has to take on the dummy hand. If he beats the dummy hand, he collects the pot. But if he loses, he has to *double* the pot. And not only that, anybody who stayed in and lost has to double the pot.

So you can see how quickly the pot can grow. Let's say the pot is at $5 and two players stay in. One of them loses to the other. And then the winner loses to the dummy hand. That means both players have lost, and they each have to double the pot. Each of them puts up $10. This means the pot will be $25 before everybody antes up 25 cents for the next hand.

There were about six guys playing on the night this particular game of Guts took place. One of the guys, the way Tim describes him, was like the Tom Breitling of Bishop Gorman High School. Nicest guy in the world, but square as a box. He was everybody's friend, and peer pressure pushed him into the game. His name is Mike Demman.

The game was way over Mike's head, and on this night it was way over everybody's head. Nobody was winning, and the pot built up quickly. Once it got into the hundreds, everybody started playing conservatively because the money on the table was more than just about anybody had.

Nobody was staying in the game. It was easier to throw down your cards, toss in another quarter, and pray for two aces. But nobody got *any* good cards, the pot kept building, and it got to be two o'clock in the morning.

Finally, with $800 in the pot, the cards were dealt and it came time for Mike Demman to decide if he was in or out. Tension filled his face and everyone could see it.

"Oh, man," His voice was tortured. "I don't know what to do."

He was completely sincere, and everyone could feel his agony. He wasn't the type of guy to bluff. Even if he could, it didn't matter. There's little bluffing in Guts because the dummy hand is waiting to be played. You can't trick the dummy hand out of the game.

Finally, Mike Demman decided. "Damn!" He threw down his cards. "I'm out."

Everybody else went out, too. Naturally, everybody was curious about Mike's hand. So they asked him to turn over his cards.

Two jacks.

Tim went berserk. "What! Are you crazy! How could you not stay in?"

Everybody piled on.

"You pussy!"

"How could you go out!"

"What the fuck is the matter with you?"

Then the dummy cards were turned over.

Once Mike saw he would've won the pot, his humiliation turned to devastation. At that point, everybody *really* let him have it. Tim was beside himself.

"Two jacks! Two jacks! What were you thinkin'? Why would you even need to think? It's impossible to lose!"

Mike Demman left the table and ran outside.

Tim felt bad for him. He really liked Mike, and if anybody was going to win the pot besides himself, he would've liked for Mike to win it.

Winning an $800 pot at two in the morning would have been a huge moment in the life of a square in the tenth grade.

So Tim went outside to talk to Mike. When he got there, he found Mike Demman crying.

"What do you mean it was impossible that I could lose?" Mike said. "Someone else could have had queens, kings, or aces. Don't you understand? If I'd lost, I would've owed $1,600.

And I don't have $1,600!"

"Nobody has $1,600!" Tim said. "That's not the point! You could've asked me to lend you the money. If I didn't have it, you could've tried to get it somewhere else. But two jacks in a game of Guts, you *gotta* stay in."

Well, if you haven't gotten the point by this point. That's *Tim*.

But *that* Tim didn't have any responsibility on his shoulders. That Tim didn't have to worry about making decisions on a $215 million property that would impact a lot of people. That Tim could just be Tim.

Now, he was my partner. Every decision he made had an impact on my life and affected investments made by Perry, Andre, and Chuck Mathewson. Every decision he made had an impact on the jobs of The Nugget senior execs planning to send their kids to college. Every decision he made rippled from our personal assistant, Zach, all the way out to Reinaldo the window washer.

So when those parentheses started to appear on the DOR, Tim had to take into account that I didn't have the same lining in my stomach that he had in his. In some way, in the world of gambling, that made Tim less than *Tim*.

He knew he was in a fight with Mr. Royalty every time the guy bobbed and weaved to the craps table. The way that Mr. Royalty was playing, it was like going up against Mike Tyson in his prime.

Mr. Royalty was not coming to play a congenial game. There was a viciousness in the way he played that went way beyond money. He played to hurt. There was a reason for this just as there was a reason somewhere in Mike Tyson's past that led him to want to smash an opponent's nose through the back of his head.

Years before, after a nice run through the casinos, Mr. Royalty suffered a reversal of fortune and went broke. Las Vegas is a small town, and word got around. When he went bust, he tried to negotiate discounts on his markers like a lot of gamblers. But that's something usually done in advance. The casinos had him by the jugular, and they wouldn't allow any discounts after he'd lost. Word is that a lien was placed on his home and that every cent was wrung out of him.

Yeah, Mr. Royalty had lost the money. But it must've done something to his head seeing the same people who'd been treating him like a king to get his action suddenly turn on him like sharks at the scent of blood. I never knew him personally, but I heard enough about him to know that he had a wife and kids. Word was, the wringer the casinos put him through also put the squeeze on his family, too. Apparently, Mr. Royalty never forgot.

A true gambler never goes bust. Everybody else might see him as busted. But *he* never does. *He* sees himself as temporarily out of ammunition. Mr. Royalty was a smart guy. He earned some money, cleared away his debts, and when he came back to the casino floor, it wasn't about table games. It was about payback.

You're gonna act like my friends and then try to put my kids in a cardboard box? Okay, that's how we'll play the game.

The higher the limits, the harder he hit. Once he got The House in the hole, he would corner it without remorse, make it fight by his rules, or else he'd take his business elsewhere. He'd issue ultimatums that the box man couldn't leave to take a piss while he was rolling. Screw the box man! Mr. Royalty wasn't going to have *his* rhythm interrupted by some bastard's prostate. If the box man needed to take a piss, let *him* sit there and swallow the pain.

Like I say, I never met the guy. But when you understand a little of the story beneath the story, you get some insight as to why Mr. Royalty might throw tips in the air to watch people in the casino jump for them as if they were dogs. Pure and simple: He wanted to make every fucking casino in Las Vegas pay.

Tim may have had the numbers on his side against Mr. Royalty. But a part of him was also thinking about the responsibilities of owning a $215 million casino. That part of him was thinking about protecting me. In a boxing ring, a fighter making a simple glance over to a friend was the finger snap a Mike Tyson would need to knock a man's nose through the back of his head. The same applied on the casino floor.

Tim began to have the shittiest feeling in the world that a gambler like *Tim* could possibly feel. He felt like Mike Demman did at two in the morning with two jacks and an $800 pot in front of him.

It was a new feeling, this wavering, and Tim didn't know what to do with it. For the first time in his life as a gambler, Tim found himself frightened. It wasn't the kind of fear that made him *start* drinking. It was the kind of fear that made him *stop*. No more wine and heavy dinners. He began to chug Red Bull energy drinks and smoke cigarette after cigarette.

It was a relief when he got word that Jack Binion was having lunch in one of our restaurants—and he headed over to see him. If there were anybody in the world who could understand what he was going through, it would be the son of Benny Binion.

Jack Binion had seen it all. His last name was synonymous with the word "gamble." He'd come to Vegas as a little boy, sleeping on the blanket that covered the two million bucks his father had stashed in the back of his Cadillac. And he could tell you stories from a day when a cheater like Shoeshine Nick was grazed in the neck with a gunshot in an alley to discourage him from ever walking through the doors of The Nugget again. Jack knew what kind of stomach it took to offer a man the chance to bet as much as he wished so long as it was his first bet. He knew what it was like to watch his casino lose every one of its $5,000 chocolate-colored chips to Archie Karas during The Run. He knew what it was like to store Archie's chips in the Horseshoe's security vault, and what it was like to have to ask Archie to cash in some of the chips because there were so many in the vault that there weren't enough on the casino floor. There was one more thing Jack Binion knew. He knew what it was like to watch Archie Karas ultimately lose every chip that he'd won.

Yes, Jack Binion was the right guy to talk to—especially since Mr. Royalty had recently beaten *his* casino out of $2 million.

"It's just impossible for this guy to win like he's winning," Tim said to Jack. "I don't think he's cheating. You must have checked out the tapes on this guy. Are you a million percent sure that nothing's up? No loaded dice. Nothing."

"Our best people have looked at it," Jack said. "He's not doing anything wrong. He's just lucky."

"Jeeezus, Jack, what the hell? Every time this guy walks through the door he beats us for at least a half million. How far should I let this guy go? Are you going to let him keep playing?"

"Of course, I'm gonna keep letting him play!"

"I don't know. Everybody else, I'm thrilled to see come through the door. This guy, I'm getting scared of. I just don't understand it."

"Well," Jack said, "you can only go as far as your bankroll allows you. On a mathematical basis, you let him play. But if you can't afford it, that's another story."

That was the worst part. Jack could stand by the math. He could tell Tim what it took to stomach The Run. But as he said good-bye, Tim realized that the essence of the conversation came down to a single question that only he could answer. How big are your balls?

That question swelled larger and larger over the coming days to the point of bursting on the night Mr. Royalty made twenty-two straight passes at the craps table and ran his winnings on us up to $8 million.

If *I* felt like throwing up watching those rolls in the surveillance room, you can only imagine what it felt like to be Tim that night. In some ways, it must've been like being Mike Demman deciding to go in with two jacks, then turning up the dummy cards and finding out he'd lost to two queens. Twenty-two times in a row!

Ironically, the losing roll that ended Mr. Royalty's streak was the knockout punch. That's when Mr. Royalty decided to pull in his chips and simply walk out the door with his two million. We were left stunned like the victims of a hit-and-run.

Remember, we were not a corporation with billions in resources. When you lose $8 million to a player in full view of your employees, they're going to talk. They're going to start to wonder how far you'll let the losses go, what'll happen if the losses go too far, and what you'll do if The House starts to fall. They're going to wonder if you're prepared to reach into your own pockets to hold it up.

Tim, Ed, and I knew there was no danger of missing an upcoming $7.5 million interest payment. But if we kept letting Mr. Royalty play, and he beat us for another $7.5 or $15 million, what would we do then? Mr. Royalty could've wiped out our entire fortune if the streak continued. Archie Karas's winning streak lasted for a year.

The next morning, when Tim failed to show up for an executive meeting, I began to think about a strategy going forward, and not only that, but about how The Nugget might evolve. Every successful casino evolves into a clear vision. The volatility in our DOR was demanding that we figure out ours.

Lorenzo and Frank's philosophy was 180 degrees away from Tim's. There was no gamble in their Station Casinos. Their casinos were built for the enjoyment of locals who worked in the industry and lived in Vegas. Station Casinos made money off of every aspect of their business, and their slot machines churned out predictable profits night after night. There was no risk in slot machines. The slots never lost. They never called in sick. They never gave anybody any trouble. They were strong and steady, the foundation of an empire.

Guys like Kirk Kerkorian and Steve Wynn had so many hotels and big players coming in and betting big money that someone like Mr. Royalty could never make a dent in their DOR. Twenty guys could be betting like Mr. Royalty, and it didn't matter. Kerkorian and Wynn had volume on their side. So much volume, their table games had become as predictable as slot machines. That was earned money. While they worked hard for it, they didn't have to sweat it.

A part of Tim wanted to sweat it, needed to sweat it. "Money won," he'd tell you, "is twice as sweet as money earned."

He loved the risks that came with deciding player limits, and he loved the tingle that came with watching his risks play out. Exchanging that for a predictable profit might put Tim in a place that he really didn't want to be.

"Do you know what the worst thing there is for a gambler, Tom?" he once told me. "The absolute worst thing. A nuclear war with plagues and famine doesn't compare to what a gambler is really scared of. To a gambler, nothing is worse than being out of action. Because if you're out of action, you might as well be dead."

The next day, when Tim failed to show up for that morning meeting, the calls started coming.

"Where's Tim?"

"Where's Tim?"

"Where's Tim?"

"Where's Tim?"

"Where's Tim?"

"Where's Tim?"

I had to find him. Along the way, I had to search for myself, too.

I found Tim lying in a bed in the Steve Wynn Suite. He looked like a gambler who hadn't slept in a week. He hadn't shaved, and the weight he'd lost was really apparent. There were ashtrays loaded with cigarette butts around the room. More scattered cans of Red Bull. The television was on.

I pulled a chair up next to the bed. After "How you doin'?" we said little. For a long time, we said nothing at all. The strangest part about the silence is how close I began to feel to him. So close that at one point I looked at the fatigue in his face and saw myself.

I remembered a night at Caesars Palace a few years after I'd moved to Vegas. Tim had taught me to gamble, and we were starting to make enough money in our reservation business for me to step out and take a risk.

I got up $10,000 at a blackjack table, went down $5,000, and got back up $10,000. It was big money for me. The energy swirled around me, and I was completely into the game. That was the night when I understood why people travel thousands of miles to come to Las Vegas.

"Hey," Tim said, "there's a guy singing Sinatra in the lounge. You want to go check him out? We'll get a drink and call it a night."

"No, no," I told him. I was down $10,000 at that point, and I wanted it back and more. "I want to stay. I'm feelin' it tonight."

"Tom, c'mon."

"No, I'm tellin' you. I'm feelin' it tonight."

"Don't stay up all night, Tom; We've got to work in the morning."

"You go. I'm gonna play."

Tim left, and by five in the morning I'd lost my entire credit limit of $25,000.

When I arrived to work on no sleep, he didn't have to ask a single question.

"You fuckin' dummy," he said.

It's always easier for somebody else to see the dark side of Vegas when it's on your face than it is with your own eyes. Which is why there's nothing better in Las Vegas than having a partner you can trust.

At one point, I picked up a pillow and tossed it at Tim to lift him out of his funk.

"Look," I told him, "I don't care about the money. I just don't want to see you like this. I want to see you healthy. Right now, that's all I care about."

But really, a lot of the time was spent in silence. When you're that close, you don't have to say much anyway.

CHAPTER 15

PROJECT GOLDFISH

The piano tune that changed everything came a few months later.

Tim had set the ring on his cell phone to play the theme song from the movie *The Sting*. He loved the ragtime piano melody that came to be synonymous with Paul Newman and Robert Redford pulling off an elaborate con. Given everything that would transpire, maybe the tune was fitting. Everything that followed over the next few weeks sure played out like a movie.

The New Year had, just a few days before, rung in 2005. We were taking some time off at Tim's beach house in California to rejuvenate and plan. Funny, that they call these sorts of business vacations retreats even though they're about looking ahead. A few of us were eating lunch at a restaurant when the melody for *The Sting* started to jingle. Tim pulled out his cell phone, said hello, and "Hey, how you doin'?" Then his expression grew serious.

Maybe the seriousness stood out even more than usual because we were as relaxed as we'd been in months.

The dreaded parentheses on our DOR immediately vanished after we'd decided not to give Mr. Royalty the game he'd wanted and pulled back on our risk all around the casino. Mr. Royalty howled and called us pussies when we took away his special limits. That was predictable. But as much as it was a dagger in Tim's heart to watch Mr. Royalty walk away with our $8 million when he knew we had the best of it, there was salve to be found every morning in the climbing numbers on the DOR.

We'd turned our focus away from the million-dollar whales and honed in on the $100,000 gamblers and loyal customers. It wasn't like the porterhouse on Tim's plate had been traded for a ham sandwich. But I knew this would be a huge adjustment for Tim, and I looked for a place where he could channel his energy. Fortunately, there was one. I'd been formulating expansion plans, and I sensed we'd have a blast working on the project together. Not only that, but focusing on these plans might give Tim the chance to turn himself from The Gambler into The Creator. It was like I was asking Tim to shift from being Jack Binion to Steve Wynn. Tim does love architecture, and he threw himself into it.

We commissioned a rendering of a 1,000-room tower and a new showroom, and we looked into buying and leasing adjacent property. We set up three stages of expansion calling for investments of $80 million, $180 million, and ultimately $250 million. Just when I thought Tim *was* morphing into Steve Wynn, he startled me by also taking on the traits of Lorenzo and Frank's dad.

Mr. Fertitta was famous for his inclusiveness. He always made the final decision, but he built his company by letting anyone who worked for him have a say if they had an idea that could make the company better. Tim started to call meetings with our executives and staff and challenge them to find ways to increase revenues and reduce costs. He pushed people to think differently, and, just like Mr. Fertitta, he inspired great ideas. The senior execs who were so jittery over the parentheses on the DOR became reengaged. I found myself amazed watching Tim become a hybrid of Steve Wynn and Frank Fertitta Jr.

Business was booming, and the future couldn't have looked better when Tim lifted up his second finger to say "excuse me" to everyone at the table and stood to leave.

For a second I wondered if something had happened to a member of his family. But Tim often got calls from The Nugget with questions or problems. On rare occasions, he liked to have those conversations in private where he could think clearly.

The three of us who remained at the table—our assistant, Zach, Ed, and I—watched Tim walk over to an isolated stool at the bar and sit. It was impossible to know what was up, and our conversation slowly returned to the NFL playoffs.

Anyway, the same finger that had gone up to say "excuse me" came down on my shoulder a few minutes later.

"Hey," Tim said to Ed and me, "I've gotta talk to you guys."

We walked back to the bar, and I couldn't imagine what was up.

"That was Tilman Fertitta on the phone."

Tilman Fertitta is a distant cousin to Frank and Lorenzo. He runs a company called Landry's Restaurants Inc.—a big company. There are more than three hundred restaurants under Tilman's wingspan. We'd been in contact with Tilman months earlier when we put The Nugget's smaller property in Laughlin up for sale to raise cash and focus our attention on our operation in Vegas. When a higher bidder entered the picture, Tilman pulled out. The deal eventually dissolved, and we held onto the property. So I wondered why Tilman would be calling now.

"Tilman just offered us $275 million for The Nugget in Vegas."

That was $55 million more than we'd bought it for after fees less than a year earlier.

"Holy shit!" was all I could say.

"In fact," Tim said, "he wants to send his private jet and fly us to Houston to meet with him tonight or tomorrow."

It was as if Tim had just been plugged into a socket and recharged. I felt like I'd stuck my finger into a socket, too. Only I kind of stood there in shock. I wasn't just shocked by the offer. I was also taken back by the electricity coming off Tim. Though I immediately realized that Tim thought it could be a great deal, I didn't have time to process all the reasons why he might've been so amped.

But I should have remembered one of Tim's favorite sayings. "Money won is *twice as sweet* as money earned." For the last three months of 2004, Tim had been earning his money. The moment he walked back from the bar at lunch, twice-as-sweet Tim was back.

Not only was a deal in play. But in a fraction of an instant, Tim sensed that the number Tilman Fertitta had cast our way— $275 million—meant that we already had the best of it. And that was just the *first* offer. Of course, that number was merely a fishhook for Tilman. We had absolutely no plans to sell The Nugget, and Tilman knew he needed to throw out a number like that to reel us to the table.

"Let's go," Tim said.

He was all set to dial the phone and have Tilman send his company jet. I wasn't surprised that Tim wanted to talk with

Tilman. You have to listen to an offer like that. But a part of me couldn't get my head around why Tim seemed so eager to sell his dream.

"Whoa, whoa, whoa," Ed said. His eyes had opened wide at first. But he quickly adjusted to the news. "You're on a retreat here."

Tim came back with one of his favorite Sinatra lines. "There will be plenty of time to rest when we're dead." Then he added, "I say we go to Houston!"

"Don't go jumping on a plane right away just because he asked you to," Ed said. "Tell him that we might be able to come in a couple of days."

Ed was right. We needed to digest this.

We went to see a movie about Bobby Darin as we had planned. The movie made me realize just how stunned I was. I simply couldn't pay attention to the screen. I sat in my seat trying to make sense of it all. Did I really want to sell The Nugget?

I loved The Nugget. I loved the fact that I could find Kirby Puckett, my grandmother's favorite Minnesota Twin, sitting at a table in one of our restaurants, and that I could go over and say hello, not as an autograph seeker, but as the owner of the hotel who could buy him dinner in gratitude for all the great moments he'd given my family. I loved when Coach K—the guy who coached my heroes as a kid—and his family came by. I loved getting to know Tony and Danny Bennett, and going on stage to sing with the Barenaked Ladies. I loved being able to have the singer who often graced our ballroom, Martin Nievera, serenade my parents at a Hawaiian-themed fortieth anniversary party at 4:04 PM on 4/04/04. I loved meeting the mayor and confronting the challenge of elevating the atmosphere downtown. I loved turning the place around after the reality show and showing the writer who called us Home Alone on Fremont Street that we were not alone. Every room was booked. I loved hosting a gala for Andre Agassi's foundation, and seeing the gratitude in his eyes when we made our hotel feel just like his home.

What could I buy with $55 million that was going to be better than all that? Besides, I was just getting over the learning curve and ready to do some serious wingin' and dingin'.

I really needed to talk it out with Tim. The ironies were already starting. Usually, Tim is the one always talking through a movie. The film might be in the middle of the opening credits when Tim would start moaning. "I don't know what the hell's going on in this movie. Does *anybody* know what's going on?" And when a climactic moment was approaching, you could lay 3-1 he'd say, "Watch this! Watch this! I'll bet you he gets it *right here*!" All around, people would be shushing and pleading for quiet. He was at it again during the Bobby Darin story, snapping his fingers to "Mack the Knife" and crooning along.

Only this time, *I* couldn't help myself. "Tim," I asked during a quiet moment in the film, "do you really think selling is the right thing?"

Tim turned toward me suddenly. "Hey, Tom," he said in exasperation. "Can I *please* watch the movie?"

As the afternoon turned to evening and we considered the deal's possibilities, I was conflicted, wanting to hit the brakes even as everyone grew more and more excited. Our pal Naaygs joined us for dinner. When we told him about the offer, he was flabbergasted.

"You guys were born under a lucky star. I can't believe it!" he shouted to the heavens. "This is a score! A *score*! There's nothing to think about here. Take the money!"

We talked it over. Then Tim called Tilman back and told

him that we could come to Houston in a couple of days.

"Just let me know when," Tilman said. "I'll have the plane ready whenever you want it."

Two days later, Tilman's plane picked us up in California. Having been through the scrutiny of a gaming license investigation, we got a little carried away as we headed east. We began to wonder if the flight crew was listening in on our conversations and if our seats were bugged. It was in this spirit that we produced the comical code name for our mission: Project Goldfish. Gold for The Golden Nugget. Fish for the theme behind Tilman Fertitta's most well-known restaurant, Landry's Seafood House.

Tilman's plane stopped in Las Vegas so that we could get a change of clothes. Also, we knew that if we were going fishing, we didn't want to end up being the fish. It was obvious that Tilman had thrown the $275 million out as bait, so Tim wanted to take along some bait and a fishhook himself. He had our assistant, Zach, go to The Nugget and get the architects' drawings of our expansion plans. This would show that we had huge aspirations and weren't at all eager to sell.

If you were watching all this in a movie, there was a little scene that would play out here to tip off the future. It would be very innocent and flit by in a couple of seconds. A good director would make it very subtle. The scene took place at the airport in Las Vegas. While waiting for us to get that change of clothes, the pilots for Tilman Fertitta's company plane crossed paths with the pilots of Frank and Lorenzo Fertitta's company plane.

Soon we landed in Houston and were picked up by Tilman's chauffeured SUV and dropped off at Tilman's baseball-themed hotel near Minute Maid Park. We met Andre and Perry's lawyer, Todd Wilson, and went out to dinner on our own at a steakhouse nearby called Vic & Anthony's. Tilman's company owned that, too.

The next morning, we went to his office.

After checking in at the reception desk, we walked over to an exhibit in the lobby—a history of Landry's Seafood House. But it was more than a history. It was a shrine to Tilman Fertitta. There were photos of Tilman everywhere. Photos of Tilman on the covers of magazines. Photos of Tilman with politicians. Photos of Tilman breaking ground on new projects. It didn't matter where in the exhibit he appeared, Tilman was always front and center.

I couldn't help but think of how different this was in comparison to Frank and Lorenzo. People always asked Lorenzo why there are no pictures of him with celebrities and dignitaries in his office—and to this day he doesn't quite know how to answer. He just never considered putting them up. Above the desk in Frank's office is a beautiful portrait in oils that could easily be hanging in his home. It's of his dad hugging him and Lorenzo.

The more I looked at the shrine to Tilman, the more I thought about Frank and Lorenzo. One of the images that came to mind was one that I'd never actually seen, but only heard about. The field goal.

Frank is seven years older than Lorenzo and played football at Bishop Gorman. His class had gone undefeated as a junior varsity team when he was a sophomore. But the following year, when Frank and his classmates showed up as juniors for a two-day summer camp to bond with the seniors, there were huge conflicts. The seniors saw their starting jobs in jeopardy and began to freeze out the guys in Frank's class.

The lack of trust split the team apart and led to a terrible season. It was a huge lesson in Frank's life. When his class became seniors, its driving theme was that *nobody* needed to see his name in the newspaper. Everyone would work together to win the state championship. The team churned into the playoffs undefeated.

In the championship game, Bishop Gorman got down 20-0 in the first eight minutes of the game. It was a small Catholic school team playing against a large public school, and Bishop Gorman froze, as the sportscasters say, like a deer in the head-lights. But because of the sense of trust on the team, there was no finger pointing, and the team was able to regroup and battle back. At the very last second, Bishop Gorman kicked a field goal to win the game and the title.

If you ever asked Frank about the lessons that guided his family business, the field goal would be one of the first stories he'd tell you. Frank grew up teaching Lorenzo how to play foot-ball. Not *once* in his life did he ever get into a fight with his younger brother.

Well, you get the picture.

Everything about the shrine to Tilman Fertitta in front of me screamed the word "I."

Everything I knew about Frank and Lorenzo, their family, and their business expressed the word "we" without them even having to say it.

After a few minutes, Tim, Ed, Zach, Todd, and I were ush-ered upstairs to the hugest office I've ever seen. It had to be sixty feet long by thirty feet wide with twenty-foot ceilings. There was room enough for three offices, and it easily contained a large desk, a large sitting area, and a large conference table.

"Gentleman, gentleman, how y'all doin'? Welcome. Wel-come." Tilman Fertitta greeted us with a Texas-sized helping of charisma. This was a guy who started out selling vitamins, moved on to hotels, restaurants, and real estate, and created a $700 million empire.

We sat at the conference table, went through the customary pleasantries, and then Tilman explained why he'd made the offer and flown us in. He wanted to grow his company, he said, and at the same time lift his stock price. He said he could go out and build a large number of new restaurants for between $250 and $275 million, but that there was a more efficient way to grow—to buy a gaming company.

This made perfect sense. Gaming companies are valued more highly than restaurants because they have better margins and higher cash flow. So Tilman could expand his company much more rapidly by buying The Nugget. At the same time, he'd attach a higher multiple to his stock and create a company with a broader base.

Pulling this off, Tilman continued, was not going to be a problem. He said he'd already done a debt deal and raised hundreds of millions of dollars for just this purpose. His tone made you think he could pull the cash out of one of his desk drawers.

If Donald Trump lived in Texas, he'd be Tilman Fertitta. Everything about Tilman's presentation made the word "large" larger than large. He had an uncanny way of finding just the right opening to point out that his home had more square footage than any other home in the most exclusive of neighborhoods. On one hand, it didn't make sense. Why tell people you wanted to do a deal with how rich you are? It could only encourage them to ask you for more money. On the other hand, his method was obviously successful. Maybe the idea was to make us feel a sense of awe in his presence.

Whatever you think of the guy, a part of you has to respect him. He'd come up with nothing and made it all by himself. He was one smooth salesman. His remarks easily transitioned into compliments about what we'd done with The Golden Nugget—which gave him an opening to ask about us.

What he really wanted was to see our company's numbers. He wanted to make an offer that wasn't just bait on a fishhook. He also wanted to mesmerize us if he could and move the process as quickly as possible. That way, we wouldn't have the time or the inclination to open the door to other bidders. The more bidders, the more Tilman knew he'd have to pay.

We began talking up The Nugget, but we were a little elusive.

Then came the cigarette that changed everything.

Tim wanted to smoke, and he asked if he could do so on Tilman's balcony.

"Let me join you," Tilman said.

They were gone for about fifteen minutes. At the time, I didn't hear a word that was said. But looking back, those few moments set a lot of different forces in motion.

"Of course," Tilman told Tim on that balcony, "we'd like to keep all this confidential." Tim immediately understood the ramifications of this sentence. Underneath "we don't want any-body to know about this" was really "you're not going to tell Frank and Lorenzo, are you?"

Tim wasn't sure how much Tilman knew about our rela-tionship with Frank and Lorenzo. But at that moment, he had two thoughts. The first was that there was no amount of money that could possibly stop him from telling Lorenzo and Frank. Second, he knew that Tilman's obsession with competing in his cousins' backyard would be to our advantage.

"Tilman, there's no way I'm going to make a deal with you for The Nugget and not tell Frank and Lorenzo," Tim said. "They're not going to find out by picking up a newspaper."

If that pushed Tilman back, Tim drew him closer when they returned to the conference table. He pulled out the archi-tectural drawings and began describing the details behind the 1,000-room tower and the new showroom.

As Tim became more and more animated, Tilman became more and more excited. He couldn't stay seated. When he

212 * DOUBLE OR NOTHING

began to wander around the table, an image flashed through my mind. It was the image of Barry Diller. Diller used to get up and pace around when he was excited during the negotiations with some of us on Expedia's board of directors over the company's purchase price.

Tilman and Barry Diller didn't look anything alike. Barry walked around with a sweater draped over his shoulders. Tilman was casual in a mock turtleneck and slacks. But there was a familiar scent in the air, and I got a good whiff of it. It was the scent of a deal junkie.

Tim's phone may not have been ringing—but I could hear the theme song to *The Sting*. I started to wonder just who was going to get stung.

Tim became more and more enthused as he explained how the enhanced hotel in Vegas would be a springboard for Golden Nuggets around the country. The more excited he got, the more my face turned to stone. The affable guy who could learn the first name of your kids on a twenty-story elevator ride stopped talking. There was something about Tilman I just didn't trust.

By the end of the meeting, though, Tilman had gotten what he wanted. We agreed to show him our numbers so he could make a solid offer. And I definitely sensed that Tim was leaning his way.

When Tilman offered his helicopter to fly us to the airport, it seemed as if he was determined to keep the home court advantage even after we left his office. I told him that wouldn't be necessary because I had to go back to the hotel and pick up my clothes.

"Ohhhh, Tom, a helicopter ride would be great!" Tim said in front of Tilman. "We could beat all the traffic!"

If there was ever a time I wanted to be stuck in traffic, it was precisely that moment. I was in no hurry to go anywhere.

I just couldn't understand why Tim was so eager to sell his dream. Had he burnt himself out? It seemed like he'd recovered from the loss to Mr. Royalty, but maybe he needed more time. As I chewed on all this, I also worked over my doubts about whether or not I wanted to sell, and whether $275 million was the appropriate price.

I'd begun to get a feeling that the number should be even higher. After all, we'd put a lot into the property. There'd been an amazing upsurge in the Las Vegas real estate market over the last year. Besides, Tilman was offering a deal based on our cash flow. If our flow was higher by the time he got a gaming license and was approved to make the transaction, he said, his price could climb as high as $290 million. Well then, as long as he brought it up, maybe $290 million was where the negotiations should start. It was time to do some serious research about that number. It was time for some due diligence. As usual, my due diligence drove Tim crazy. Needless to say, it wasn't long before Tim and I had a meltdown.

"Look, Tom, you don't need a complex formula here. This deal offers to put more in our pockets in one day than we could have hoped to make over the next six years. And that's with everything at The Nugget going *perfectly* over all that time."

"Tim, all I'm saying is that this decision should be made with extreme care. I don't want to look back a year or two from now with regrets. This was your dream, remember?"

"That's right, Tom, I'm the one who wanted to buy the casino in the first place. I'm the one who went through all that crap to get the gaming license."

"Oh, and I haven't been with you every step of the way? Screw that!"

"Tom, why are you being so hardheaded and stubborn? Why are you holding us back?"

"All I'm saying is that this is worthy of a fair discussion. There's no reason to sell if we don't get the right price. We've put our lives into that hotel, and he's got to pay big-time to take our names off it."

"Tom, are you looking for a way to get a higher price, or a way to not do the deal?"

"All I'm saying is we should take our time and think this through. Are we going to let Tilman determine the price? Maybe *we* should start at $290 million."

"Tom, I'm not rolling over and handing him the keys for $275 million. It's his *first* offer. Can't you see? He's obsessed with getting into Vegas. A guy who builds his own shrines will pay whatever it takes. Look, we've got a chance to make a big score here. Why slow it down? Why fuck it up?"

They say that Abbott and Costello hated each other. They say that when Abbott was scripted to hit Costello during their comedy routines, he really belted him. But in spite of the language and the screaming, our meltdowns were never personal. They were simply our way of trying to find the best direction to move forward—though a moment would occur a few weeks later that would take our friendship to the brink.

At this point we were the gas pedal and the brake pedal simultaneously punched to the floor. The smell in the air was burning rubber.

We'd come full circle. Only a year before, Tim wanted to pay more money than I felt comfortable with to buy a casino, and I had to slow him down to the point where The Nugget became available at a price that was right for us. Now, if I did want to sell, I felt like I had to slow him down to get the price as high as Tilman would possibly go.

Anyway, the argument was the storm before the calm— before the calm before the storm.

The calm came when Tim called Lorenzo and asked him to swing by The Nugget to talk about something he didn't want to discuss over the phone. Naturally, Lorenzo wondered what was going on and drove over right away. When he sat down with Tim, he was both startled and not surprised at the same time.

He'd heard rumors that Tilman wanted to get into gaming and he knew about Tilman's interest in The Nugget in Laughlin. Word was swirling around town that Tilman was looking at the Riviera on The Strip. What astounded Lorenzo was that Tilman had set his sights on our property.

When the shock subsided, Lorenzo could only smile. How could he not be happy when his friends were about to make a huge score?

The next morning, Lorenzo phoned Frank to tell him everything.

Before he could finish all the details, Frank had already made some mental valuations and calculations. "At that price," he said, "*we* should buy it."

CHAPTER 16

THE ODDS COUPLE

There was a moment when I first moved to Las Vegas that makes me realize just how outlandish the dream to own a casino had become. Back then, Tim was still driving a crappy Chevy, and I was still the square from Barnsville. We'd just become partners in his hotel reservation business when we drove down The Strip and passed Caesars Palace. "One day," Tim turned to me and said, "we're gonna own our own hotel-casino."

I stared up at Caesars and started laughing. Tim got pissed.

But what were the odds that a couple of guys making $25,000 a year could pull something like that off? What were the odds that we'd go on to buy The Golden Nugget and then have a chance to sell it in less than a year for more than $50 million in profit? And what were the odds that the two companies competing for The Nugget would be run by cousins with the last name Fertitta?

When news reached me that Frank and Lorenzo were interested in buying The Nugget, I was taken aback. Just as wide-eyed as I was on the day when Tim first told me about Tilman's offer. Only this time, another emotion flooded through me—relaxation.

All the tension drained out of me, and everything fell into place.

I immediately adjusted to the fact that we were going to sell. My fears that Tim might be seeing the sale as an easy way out after the beating we'd absorbed from Mr. Royalty were gone. They'd been pushed aside by Perry's reaction. He, too, sensed the twice-as-sweet nature of the deal. I'd also come to understand Tim's thinking a little better after Andre reacted to the idea of selling with disbelief.

Andre placed a huge value on the adrenaline that came with the partnership and the place. To him, it was like he was surfing with friends who suddenly wanted to quit when he couldn't wait to see what the next wave looked like. "Don't be a bitch!" he said to Tim.

"Andre, this is only the first offer, and it's probably more money than we can make in the next six years," Tim replied. "And I don't see you in the office with me ninety hours a week."

"Oh," Andre said with an understanding smile. "Then *please* sell."

What it took me time to realize is that Tim had not morphed into Steve Wynn or Mr. Fertitta. He'd turned into Kirk Kerkorian, who'll buy, sell, and rebuy the same property depending on the market value at the moment. "You cannot be emotional about a building," Kirk has said. "The only way to approach a deal is if it's good financially."

That's exactly where Tim's head was. He had already sold his baby when he sold Travelscape. Maybe Tim's dream of owning a casino had been achieved the day he let the roulette player put down the bet that nobody else in Las Vegas would take. It wasn't going to get any better than that for Tim at The Nugget—especially now that the limits had been strapped down.

If Lorenzo and Frank were doing the buying, everything would be as comfortable as a handshake.

With the purchase price in Tilman's deal memo tied to present and future cash flow, Landry's $275 million offer was squishy. There really wasn't an exact number, and from our perspective, our cash flow was and would be lower than ideal. That was because of the $8 million loss to Mr. Royalty in the third quarter, a huge marketing budget put in place to build a long-term business, and a lot of other transitional costs. Our marketing budget was three times what it would've been if we had planned on selling. That was a huge advantage for Tilman when he tied the deal to cash flow and there would be no way we could make up for it in the short term. Everybody knows that a business doesn't operate at maximum efficiency and profitability when there's a Just Sold sign on the property and it's transitioning owners. All these abnormalities were being held against us.

There were no ties to cash flow in Lorenzo and Frank's offer of $275 million, and there was nothing squishy about it.

Even if you stripped away the friendship and the solid nature of their offer, there were other good reasons to complete the deal with them. Frank and Lorenzo already had a gaming license in the state of Nevada. It might take Tilman more than a year to go through the arduous licensing procedure—and there were no guarantees that he'd get one. At the very least, the licensing process would hold up the transfer of property to Tilman for about a year.

What's more, Frank and Lorenzo's company has been

ranked by *Fortune* magazine as the eighteenth-best company to work for in America. That would be reassuring to anyone employed at The Nugget. The environment was so pleasant at Station Casinos that employees saw no reason to unionize.

In fact, this was one of the few sticking points and complications. The Golden Nugget *was* unionized, so Frank and Lorenzo needed time to figure out how a hotel with unions would be merged into their existing structure. Until this was settled, we needed to figure out a way to keep Tilman at a distance without cutting him loose.

In the meantime, we had lawyers start the preliminary work. We tentatively agreed to sell The Nugget to Station Casinos for $275 million. If Tilman pushed that number higher, the price would *always* be $20 million less than Landry's best offer. It was worth the $20 million to us to sell to friends whom we could trust, who had a gaming license, and who could take over the property almost immediately. In my mind, taking $275 million from Frank and Lorenzo wasn't equivalent to taking $295 million from Tilman. It was better.

Lorenzo, Tim, Frank, and I shook hands. There's been more friction between the four of us fighting over a dinner check than there was in working out the basic details of this deal. These were not handshakes. These were handshakes that turned into embraces.

The next day, Tim opened a suite at The Nugget so that Station's executives and analysts could examine our numbers. When a spy (there's no other way to describe the bastard) in our hotel saw these execs come through the lobby, it was only minutes before Tilman was on the phone and howling.

So what? Tim responded. We didn't have a deal with you.

It may have been all settled between us and Frank and Lorenzo.

Not so with Tilman.

A phone message came our way through an intermediary.

The message was this: "No matter what the deal is that you're working on with Station Casinos, Landry's is willing to pay $20 million more. *And,* no matter what Station Casinos offers in the future, Landry's *will always* be willing to pay $20 million more."

The words must've sounded bold and dramatic when first proposed in Houston. But Tilman could have no idea that our agreement with Frank and Lorenzo stipulated that we'd sell to Station's for $20 million *less* than any offer Tilman made.

The message reached Ed, our point person and buffer on the deal, late at night through the intermediary. The intermediary asked Ed to promise that he'd get the message to Tim and me.

Tim was sleeping at the time. He was awakened by a piano tinkling the ragtime theme to *The Sting.* He reached for the phone and listened to the $20 million message. A minute later, he hung up. In Tim's world, a man's handshake is his bond. In Tim's world, the deal was done. Tim set his head on the pillow and easily drifted back to sleep.

The next morning, Ed returned the message. He told Landry's general counsel, Steve Scheinthal, that we were going ahead with plans to sell to Station Casinos. He explained that we weren't going to break our bond with Frank and Lorenzo over $20 million. Even putting aside the friendship, there were factors like the uncertainty surrounding the gaming license and the time it would take to transfer the property to Landry's that had influenced our decision. Ed thanked Landry's for its interest and closed the discussion.

Or so we thought.

Later that day, Scheinthal called Ed back.

"Has the deal been signed?" he asked.

"No," Ed said. "At this point, we're bound by our word. We're working on the final documents."

This left a slender crack, just wide enough for Tilman to slide a fax through.

Scheinthal explained to Ed that Landry's had just concluded an emergency board meeting. Landry's was prepared to offer $325 million for The Nugget. On top of that, Landry's would place $30 million in escrow. If the deal fell through because Tilman couldn't get a gaming license, the money was ours. No questions asked.

"Will you make sure the offer gets to Tim and Tom?" Scheinthal said.

"If you want me to go to Tim and Tom with this," Ed said. "I need it on paper."

The fax came through the slender crack. It said $325 million. That was more than $100 million more than we'd bought The Nugget for a year earlier, and it was $50 million more than Frank and Lorenzo had agreed to pay.

Ed told me the news.

I never thought an offer that gave you a chance to make more than $100 million dollars could make you feel so torn and shitty.

I called to tell Tim.

"We gotta go talk to Lorenzo," was all Tim could say. His voice sounded like my stomach felt.

Lorenzo was on his way to dinner with his wife, Teresa, when Tim phoned and explained that we needed to see him.

"Get the guys," Lorenzo said, "and meet us at Piero's."

"*This*," Teresa said with a knowing smile, "has all the makings of a romantic night out."

Piero's is a Vegas institution. Waiters in tuxedo jackets. A long bar. Antique pine tables. A great wine cellar. An owner who sits at your table and eats the pasta off your plate and shares your wine and has a voice that's impossible to describe and impossible to forget and a face that has proudly seen seven lifts. Sinatra used to hang at Piero's. When he was a long way away and in the mood, Frank used to have the veal milanese sent to him on the restaurant's china via his private jet. The mayor's victory party was staged at Piero's. Wayne Newton called the place home. Portions of the movie *Casino* with Robert De Niro and Joe Pesci were filmed there.

So it was fitting. The history of a friendship was about to be tested in a joint with some history to it.

Lorenzo and Teresa were already seated when Tim arrived. Ed and I were on our way. But this wasn't going to wait. Immediately, Lorenzo could see the struggle in Tim's eyes.

You've got to hand it to Tilman. He knew he had to do something dramatic to insert his "I" between our "we." That fax was more drama than anyone of us expected. Tim was hoping that Lorenzo and Frank could bump their offer up to within $20 million of the $325. That would allow us to keep our end of the deal.

When Lorenzo heard about the fax, he immediately phoned Frank. Then he turned back to Tim. There was not the slightest hesitation in his voice. "Even at $20 million less," Lorenzo said. "it's not a good deal for us."

Lorenzo could see how lousy Tim felt. When Lorenzo was captain of the Bishop Gorman football team, he made sure that when a player committed a penalty he got an emotional lift from the ten guys around him when he returned to the huddle. Though Tim had committed no penalty, that's the attitude Lorenzo took.

"This is a great offer," Lorenzo told Tim. "We're not going to stand in your way."

There was no sense of family competition with Tilman as far as Frank and Lorenzo were concerned. They only saw the deal in numbers.

"If $325 million is the number, you gotta take it," Lorenzo said, " . . . just make sure that *that's* the number."

Friendship had trumped all. But there was no celebration at the size of Tilman's offer as we walked out of Piero's. The tension was back. We were no longer dealing with friends.

"Let's call in the guys from Skadden, Arps," Tim said. "It'll cost more, but we gotta take extra precautions. This contract has to be triple, quadruple, 100 percent ironclad. If we make this deal, I don't care if Martians invade Fremont Street, Tilman's got to pay."

Skadden, Arps, Slate, Meagher and Flom is a premier law firm out of New York specializing in these types of negotiations. Everything about our dealings with Barry Diller and Microsoft had prepared us for this moment.

Even though Lorenzo and Frank had released us from our agreement, we made no quick phone call to Tilman. The next day, Tilman called Ed to find out why. As smart and wily as he is, he couldn't camouflage the scent that he *had* to win this competition with his cousins.

"Ed, this is not the way the world works," he said. "The person who pays the most should win."

Yes, he had the highest bid, but to us that wasn't the issue. We needed to know what the value of The Nugget truly was before we sold it. We could think that $325 million was a great deal and that Tilman was overpaying to beat out his cousins. But the value of The Nugget really had not been established.

There's a price of entry into Las Vegas, and I sensed that Tilman was willing to pay that price. We knew he was looking at the Riviera. Word was, the Riviera was on the block for twice the money that Tilman was offering us. Tilman was going to pay for The Nugget exactly what it was worth to his company to have it. *That* was The Nugget's value. We needed to find out what *that* number was.

There was one sure way. Ed called Landry's and explained that its $325 million offer was the highest, but that something new had come up. (Another party *was* expressing interest.) "If you guys can go up another $10 million," he said, "that would put you over the top."

Not only did we owe it to ourselves to get the best possible deal. But we remembered Barry Diller's tactics. If you sense that somebody is going to try to drop the price to the cellar down the road, it's a good idea first to try to push it through the roof.

Landry's came back and said its board would not approve another $10 million. It could only go $5 million more.

That was as high as we were going to take Tilman. Soon we would see how low he would try to take us. It was time for the boys from Skadden, Arps to come in.

Lawyers on both sides started working on the purchaser's agreement. The numbers were complicated. We didn't want the final purchase price to be linked in any way to the level of our recent earnings. We wanted Landry's to buy at the point where our profits would've been if Mr. Royalty had never set foot in the place, and if we hadn't budgeted so much on marketing to build the business up. We wanted Tilman to buy at the numbers that he would've seen with normal cash flows after our transition year. There were also complex financing terms involved, including bond payments and a $23 million revolving line of credit. If I began to describe all the twists in the deal through all the numbers on the table you'd be reading another book. And it would be a confusing book, because the numbers never really meant what the numbers seemed to be. Sure, Tilman could offer $330 million. But it wasn't *really* $330 million if it didn't assume The Nugget's $23 million revolving line of credit. There were countless ways for that $330 million to get chiseled down.

So I'm going to boil all the figures down to a simple concept.

Here it is. There's only one number that counts when you're selling a property. That's the money that goes into your bank account at the end of the deal. As precise as all the other numbers might be, they're just pencil marks on legal pads.

The lawyers worked through the points with give and take on both sides. Landry's agreed to assume The Nugget's revolving line of credit. We agreed to allow Landry's to define the purchase price on its press release. As we inched closer and closer, I remained at a strategic distance. I knew a shot was coming, and I waited for it with a poker face.

When it arrived, I still couldn't believe it.

It occurred, amazingly, in a room full of lawyers from Skadden, Arps. Neither Tim nor I was there. At the end of a long day of negotiations, Scheinthal walked to the easel at the head of the room and started reviewing the agreement. As he strolled through the purchase price, he tried to push off two bond payments at roughly $7.5 million apiece on Tim and me.

They were trying to siphon $15 million from our end of the deal in full view of Ed Borgato and some of the best lawyers in the country. Ed blinked in disbelief. "Hold on, Steve, you're forgetting something. That's not the deal at all."

Scheinthal tried for an Academy Award. "Ohhhhhh, we thought those payments were going to come out of *your* end of the deal."

Lawyers from both sides looked at each other. Ed stopped the meeting and asked Scheinthal and a few others to adjourn to another office.

"Steve," Ed cut to the chase, "what's going on?"

"Ed, we can't do the deal at this price. It's too high. Our board of directors won't allow it. We can't get a fairness opinion from our banker."

First, they had to have The Nugget. Now, they can't possibly do it. The boys from Skadden, Arps had never seen anything like it—and they'd seen it all. I was determined to remain disciplined and keep my poker face as the lawyers went home and the deal disintegrated. It was hard to know if it was simply ridiculous, or merely posturing for the next round.

"Tilman will be back," Tim said. "He's got the green felt disease. I know. I had it once myself."

The green felt disease is local lingo for a syndrome that wealthy businessmen are prone to when they get around Vegas. They just have to buy a casino. Maybe Tilman had the green felt disease. Maybe he was competing with his cousins. Maybe he'd overextended himself while getting us to the table. He was making interest payments on all the money he'd borrowed to do the deal. That had to be burning a hole in his pocket. If he really wanted The Nugget, we had him over a barrel. But playing this kind of poker with a guy like Tilman can put your stomach in knots and drive you to the nuthouse. It's like being at a poker table with a guy who won't make a decision. You're sitting there waiting for an answer. Are you in big-time? Are you out? Make up your mind already!

We figured he was going to take his shot—and he had. But now we got a call that he wanted to talk to us personally. He was flying to Vegas to work it out. We had no idea what he had in mind. Perhaps it was just as confounding for Tilman to figure *us* out.

Tim and I had assumed contradictory roles. He was the guy who wanted to surge ahead and get the deal done while I remained stone-faced and leery. While these were roles, there was some truth to them under the surface. Tim is impatient. He believes that when too many people are around the negotiating table the deal tends to slow down. So he has a tendency to go off on his own and solve problems as if he were the Lone Ranger. I needed to hold him back and exercise patience. That was one reason we'd directed all communication through Ed.

But now it was time for us to move. The good guy/bad guy routine can be useful if you're trying to keep your rival off balance. But Tilman wasn't showing us all of his cards. So Tim and I had to come together and put ours on the table.

Exactly how much money did we need to put in the bank in exchange for everything we'd put into The Nugget? It was a serious conversation, but it could have been a scene in a comical movie. That's because Tim was preparing for a part in a movie at the time, a movie we were shooting on the property. The movie was called *Bachelor Party Vegas*—and Tim had agreed to play a part as a casino owner. As he pored through spreadsheets to determine the number we needed to see in order to make the deal work, he paused again and again to rehearse his lines. But finally, we crunched all the figures down.

Tim, our partners, and I had put up $50 million of our own cash to buy the joint. Tim and I were in for $37.5 million. Andre and Perry were in for $7.5 million. And Chuck Mathewson had put up $5 million.

We could negotiate all night with Tilman about bond debt payments and the revolving line of credit, but that would only sidetrack us. We needed to stick with a single, firm number and not waver—just as we did with Expedia. The number we'd agreed upon before we were sidetracked was $163 million. That was still our number. All Tillman had to do was put $163 million in our bank accounts and The Nugget was his.

"Any regrets?" Tim asked.

"No regrets," I said.

Someone knocked on the door to tell Tim it was time for makeup.

Tim had to shoot and reshoot a scene where he snapped a pool cue in half and went wild admonishing a bunch of young guys having a bachelor party. It took about fourteen broken pool cues to get it right, and Tilman was left waiting until after midnight for the shooting to end. As soon as it did, Tim and I went to meet him.

Tilman explained that his board wouldn't let him go in for the additional $5 million. Tim became as focused as a laser. He walked to a white board and picked up a marker. And he wrote the number that mattered to us most: $163 million.

Whatever Tilman needed to do to make the final purchase price put $163 million in our bank accounts was fine by us. Whatever Tillman wanted to do on his company press release was fine by us. But *that* was the number we needed to see in our bank accounts.

There was discussion, agreement, and a casual conversation that ended at 3:00 AM.

The lawyers soon returned to The Nugget and began to move forward. We were close enough to begin sending Tilman a copy of our DOR every morning. And then a not-so-funny number appeared on the DOR midway down the page on the left-hand column.

One of our big players came into town and asked for the

high limits to which he was accustomed. It was a tough call. The limits had been strapped down ever since we stopped taking Mr. Royalty's action. But this guy wasn't Mr. Royalty. He was a nice guy, and we liked him. Tim came to me and asked what I thought we should do. We figured if he were lucky, he'd beat us for a million. If not, we'd probably take him for three million. It was almost like a last fling. We let him bet big—and the guy won a million bucks.

Naturally, the dreaded parenthesis appeared on the DOR. Of course, we could say this was abnormal, that we'd win it back and recover by the end of the month. But if you were Tilman, you woke up one morning to find out the property you were purchasing was worth a million dollars less than it was the day before. What if this pattern continued? Even Tim acknowledged that Tilman had a legitimate beef. The problem was the way he decided to cook it.

Tilman and Scheinthal walked in uninvited on a meeting between Ed and our lawyers holding a copy of that DOR.

"This is a problem. You're telling us that everything is fine, but it isn't. We're paying big money here, and we can't buy it at this price if this is what's really going on."

The more they got into it, the more heated the exchange became.

"Listen," Ed said, "there's an ebb and flow on the casino floor. It swings both ways. When you get the keys to the place you can change the odds and limits and run a different kind of a casino."

But logic is only kerosene on the fire to someone spoiling for a fight. This was not a logical confrontation, and it built to the point where Scheinthal lost it.

"Tim Poster sat right here and said that business is going good," he said. Scheinthal grabbed a pad that had a hard back, slammed it on the table and broke it in half. "Tim Poster is a fucking liar!"

Ed's fist slammed down on the table. "Don't you ever call Tim Poster a liar in this building! In fact, you can all get the fuck out right now."

Scheinthal and Tilman began to jabber that they weren't going to be taken advantage of.

"Hey," Ed came back, "let's not pretend that this is anything more than you guys trying to lower the price. You're paying a fair price—and you know it. If you don't understand the ebb and flow and economics of the casino business, maybe you ought to go back to Texas and continue to up-sell cheesecakes!"

This is just about the spot where I innocently opened the door and stepped into a room that suddenly went quiet.

"Hey, guys, what's going on?"

You couldn't help but breathe the tension.

"Tom, we're going to wrap up here in two minutes," Ed said. "Can we see you a little later?"

As much as I tried to maintain my poker face afterward when the heated back-and-forth was related to me, there's just so much a guy can take before he says "What the fuck?" I thought the deal might be dead yet again. Tim took being called a liar less personally than I did. He sensed it was just posturing. His response was to return the gesture. When a group of Landry's lawyers unpacked for their own session without knowledge of what had just gone down, Tim walked in and asked them what they were doing.

"We're going to have a meeting."

"No you're not," Tim said. "Pack up your shit and get out."

He came back to my office. It wasn't long before Scheinthal was slinking in to apologize to Tim. Tim didn't hold it against him. Then Steve asked Tim if he'd go talk to Tilman for ten minutes.

I wanted to go with Tim, but Tim thought that it was personal. "Let me go alone," he said. "Tilman wants to apologize and get things back on track. I feel it. Let's see if there's really a deal here. I'll be back in ten minutes."

Tim left. I stayed seated at my desk while Ed and the boys from Skadden, Arps paced back and forth, and Bally licked her paws and wondered what was going on. Fifteen minutes passed. No Tim. Twenty. No Tim. Half an hour. No Tim. I sensed the Lone Ranger was at it again. The boys from Skadden, Arps were not happy with the situation, whatever it was. I worked the phones to keep Andre and Perry appraised, and kept the door closed so that none of the tension would leak outside.

It's kind of crazy to describe the room in terms of tension when I think of my father landing an airplane carrying hundreds of passengers after an engine has failed. But I did get more and more anxious as the lawyers paced in front of me. They were worried that Tilman would seize on Tim's desire to sell and get the price lowered. They were worried that things were out of control. As time passed, I began to feel like a pilot whose passengers were entering the cockpit to find out just who was flying the plane. After forty-five minutes, I couldn't take it.

I headed to Tilman's suite with Ed. From behind the door, we could hear laughter ripple through the air. Like a couple of buddies who'd just returned from a morning of hunting with a sack of quail.

I rapped on the door.

There were some footsteps. Then Tilman answered.

"What's going on here?" I asked. My heart was pounding.

Tim popped up from a chair.

"Tom, Tom, everything's fine. Tilman just wanted to talk to me."

I remained expressionless as they quickly summarized their discussion. Tilman wanted to pick up the negotiations at the point where they were before he'd seen the parenthesis on that DOR. He wanted to get the deal done.

Tim, Ed, and I excused ourselves and walked through an archway in the suite to an adjoining room.

"If they're willing to do the deal at the number we agreed upon the other night," Tim asked, "are we still willing to trust the guy and do the deal?"

Trust was the last word I wanted to hear at that moment.

"You told me you were going to be back in ten minutes," I said.

Tim had taken the apology and used it to smash through the wall and get the deal done. But he was looking at a guy who didn't give a shit about money when it's measured against the word "trust."

We were no longer lucky whiz kids who hit it rich because of the Internet. We were no longer the boys who'd been chumped by Barry Diller. We were now men who'd used our very different strengths and everything at our disposal to be able to knock down the wall and finalize this deal. But in the end, we were still Tim and Tom. And so we stood a few feet apart, arms crossed, fuming.

"I'm begging you guys," Ed said. "Not now."

We walked back in the room and shook Tilman's hand. The deal was finally done.

Then we walked down the corridor in silence and headed up to Tim's office. As we did, my anger dissipated, and everything became clear to me. I'd been keeping the plane level in turbulence so that Tim could walk out on the wing. He'd gotten the deal done. Why was I giving him shit about ten minutes?

How could he think I wasn't thinking of both of us? Tim wondered. Have I *ever* not thought of both of us?

We entered Tim's office and closed the door. Bally was sitting on the couch. She looked up at us as if to say, "Hey, where have you guys been?"

We both smiled. Our smiles grew wider and wider and we burst out laughing.

And that's how we made our second $100 million.

CHAPTER 17

THE BEST OF IT

After a deal is done, there's generally a celebratory dinner on both sides.

No matter what's gone down, these meals are more fun when you're the buyer. When you sell, even if you've gotten the best of it financially, there's often a sense of melancholy that comes with the close of an adventure. When you buy, even if you've overpaid, you're lifting a glass to opportunity and toasting the possibilities of your future.

So who got the best of it?

Well, there are a lot of ways to look at it.

In a single year at The Nugget, Tim and I made a profit of $113 million. That's 226 percent on the $50 million we invested. That's more money than anyone in downtown Las Vegas has ever made faster than anyone has ever made it. In fact, it's been called the highest rate of return in such a short time span ever in the gaming industry.

I've always believed that the best deals are the ones where everybody feels like they walk away a winner.

Maybe Tilman Fertitta sits in his office at this very moment and thinks he got the best of it. The day it was announced, the deal drove up the price of Landry's shares more than 12 percent on the New York Stock Exchange. Since then, Tilman has spent $125 million renovating The Nugget. Though as I tell this story, the downtown market is in its ninth consecutive negative growth month, The Nugget's revenues are flat, and Landry's stock is at the same level it was before the deal was announced. Still, there's a huge factor that could well be in Tilman's favor. The valuations of property in Las Vegas have soared since we signed the deal on the week of the Super Bowl in 2005. They've soared to the point where Tim often says, "I don't think God could've seen what's happened to Las Vegas."

One month, we blink in disbelief when we hear that the asking price for Strip property where the Frontier sits is $36 million an acre. The next month, we're even more astonished to find out that it's been sold at that price. There's so much money floating around Wall Street and so many people with the green felt disease that these days anything less than a billion won't get you much on The Strip. If people start to look downtown as an alternative, Tilman Fertitta will be in the best possible place.

But that's just the dollars and cents of it.

As my best buddy likes to say, "You can only eat one steak at a meal." (Although he's been known to order two while seated across from a preachy vegetarian.) Tim was a much wiser man the second time around. He didn't go into a funk after he'd sold his dream. He now races twenty feet from his bedroom to the computers in his office every morning to bet on the stock market. He never said "I told you so" when he heard that Mr. Royalty lost the $8 million he'd taken from us along with just about everything else that he'd won on his streak. And he's constantly on the lookout for our next big business venture.

While waiting for our next move, I've gotten to mentor a great group of kids at the Agassi College Preparatory Academy and develop a program that assists budding entrepreneurs at the University of San Diego. I also met the love of my life. On the evening I first set eyes upon Vanessa Tarazona, her friends asked us to pose for a photo together and kept on saying, "Closer . . . closer . . . closer . . ." It never stops amazing me how we continue to grow closer by the minute. I knew it was right because my best friend told me so. So did Vanessa, when she asked that her groom and his best man be dressed in the same style of tuxedo.

Now I finish telling a story that allows me to see what my best friend and I have accomplished since we shook hands on a frozen lake.

It's kind of funny. All through the crazy negotiations with Tilman, I kept saying to Tim, "I'll believe it when I see his name in ink on paper."

But that's not the image that I took from the contract.

My most enduring memory of the contract remains the moment when I wrote *my* name in ink on the page. I did so with a gift Tim gave me just prior: a unique fountain pen.

It's called the Amerigo Vespucci pen, in honor of the Italian explorer for whom our country is named, and it's custom-made of sterling silver and mother of pearl. It came in a beautiful wooden box etched with a picture of a ship sailing with the wind at its back. I'm telling you, I was almost scared to pick this pen up. It was a huge leap from my Bic.

When I took it in my hands, I felt like John Hancock or Thomas Jefferson about to sign the Declaration of Independence. That's how I signed the contract.

I put the pen back in its leather enclosure, shut the box, and stared at the image of that ship. And I felt that we hadn't really just sold The Golden Nugget. Tim and I had just signed on to explore somewhere new.

ACKNOWLEDGMENTS

It would take more words than there are in this book to thank everyone who's helped me along on this incredible, and somewhat surreal, journey. While this may be the longest acknowledgment page you've ever encountered, trust me, I'm trying to be brief!

So, thank you to:

My parents, Fred and Carol, for all you've done to guide my life. Everything I've achieved is rooted in the gifts you've passed on: honesty and integrity, respect and hard work, flight and the passion for travel—and, of course, love and that rainbow.

Tim Poster, because even though the book is dedicated to you, a second porterhouse is needed to acknowledge your heart of gold and the impact you've had on my life. Here's a toast to the next voyage.

My wonderful wife, Vanessa Tarazona, for being beautiful

inside and out. Thanks for giving me a new way to smile each day.

My brother John, for all of your wisdom and the courage to tell me how you really feel. And my brothers Mike and Freddy, for the Piledrivers and flying high—you led by example.

My sisters, Kim, for defense; Jody, for patience; Stephanie, for Skynyrd; and Elena, for the introduction to Spanish.

Grandma Johnson, for the cribbage games; Grandpa Johnson, for his last words; Grandma Breitling, for the Frosted Flakes; and Grandpa Breitling, for the lawnmower rides.

Uncle Jack, for taking me in as his own and not laughing too hard at my naiveté.

Vicki and Frank Fertitta Jr., for their open arms and watchful eyes.

Lorenzo Fertitta, for helping me lift the brick; and Teresa, for showing me how to make a home.

Frank Fertitta III, for throwing me into the Mediterranean and showing me a world of no boundaries. And Jill, who exposed me to style.

Perry Rogers, who picks up the phone and changes the world.

Andre Agassi, for the best steak ever and the conversation that altered my life.

Ed Borgato, for slamming his fist down when it mattered, and for introducing all of us to *Cinema Paradiso*.

Todd Wilson, for the curiosity that cracked open the James Bond briefcase.

Steve and Elaine Wynn, who continue to teach us about leadership.

The Maestro, Cal Fussman, for the best ears on the planet.

Tony Bennett and Danny Bennett, for showing us the true power in a partnership and the meaning of class.

Bobby Baldwin, for the history lesson and the blessing.

Jack Binion, for asking the big question and answering it, too.

Chuck Mathewson, for trusting us enough to ante up; and Burton Cohen, who knows how to make advice seem like a good story.

Tim's mom, Nikki Xerogianes; the one and only Aunt Mary; and the legendary Uncle Jimmy, who helped make Tim *Tim*.

Captain John, for the green bananas; and Harry Kassup, for bringing the Virgin to Vegas.

Bob Martin, who taught us all how to get the best of it.

Frank Toti Sr., for his "acts of kindness"; and Frank Toti Jr., for playing the role of Tom before I arrived.

Curt Magleby, for pointing us toward the deal that changed our lives.

Edward Muncey, for being "Mr. Incredible"; and his wife, Ashley, for understanding what it takes to be *in-credible*.

The boys at Skadden, Arps: Wally Schwartz, Howard Ellin, and Todd Freed, for making sure the contract was triple, quadruple, 100 percent ironclad.

Steve Cavallaro, for margarita coupons, his extraordinary nose, and for standing his ground.

Bernie Yuman, for simply being "Bernie," because there is no other; and Gordie Brown, for the laughs.

Longtime friends Chris Bednarz, Ed Giefer, Mike Healey, Rich Dorn, and Matt Vasgersian, for keeping me humble.

Peter Wallace, for scribbling just the right notes on the napkin.

Tito Tiberti, for the backyard barbecues and bocce ball.

Bob Nagy, for the never-ending source of friendship—and amusement; and Carol, for being a saint.

Michael Reichartz, for scraping the "2" off 21st Century Investing.

Frank Sinatra, because the music lasts forever; and Matt Dusk, who reminds us of that.

Zach Conine, for leaving the hallways of Cornell to come to the roof of The Golden Nugget.

Maurice Wooden, for introducing us to every employee and making us feel at home in our home.

The legendary Johnny D.—Johnny DiCostantino—who honored us by coming out of retirement.

Pete Kaufman, for advice on how to hold up The House.

Joe Brunini, for taking a few minutes to pass on a lifetime of knowledge.

David Chesnoff, for watching our backs and insulting our fronts, and who'll get the first invite to the next roast.

Freddy Glusman, because this book and Las Vegas just wouldn't be the same without Piero's.

Richie Wilk, for bringing in the Sopranos; and Steve Cyr for hunting whales in the desert.

The 2,500 employees at The Golden Nugget, for reviving Vintage Vegas.

Larry Ruvo, for good spirits; Leor Yerushalmi, for all the bling and the perfect ring; and Patrick Lewis, because I keep my promises.

Jim and Heather Murren at the Nevada Cancer Institute, who continue to teach me how to make Vegas a better place.

The entire student body at the Andre Agassi College Preparatory Academy, including the six students that I mentor—Ricky, Jon, Cashawnda, Shaniqa, Bianca, and Simone—for their commitment and desire to take the next step.

Cedric Crear, for establishing Tim's work ethic at the fountains.

The men and women at Nellis Air Force Base and all members of the armed services for providing the freedom that allows all of us the opportunity to be entrepreneurs.

YMCA Camp Warren, where I learned to work as part of a team.

The University of San Diego, for putting me in just the right place; and Sardina's restaurant for that veal parmigiana sandwich.

Norm Clarke, Vegas's ultimate eye in the sky.

Michael Shulman, the Diva himself.

Scott Nielson, for his fine-tooth comb.

Dana White, for teaching me how to fight out of a corner.

Billy Richardson and his mom, for rolling with the punches.

Seth Shomes, for the introduction, and to Aaron Lewis for the song.

Jack Sheehan, for opening the door.

Sam Bybee, for making me aware that I only needed six hours' sleep a night; and Larry Sacknoff, for giving me my first break.

Brian Lipson, and everyone at Endeavor, who took the rollercoaster from Beverly Hills to Barnes and Noble.

Marion Maneker, for believing from the start.

Genoveva Llosa, for the meticulous editing; Ethan Friedman, for wanting to jump aboard; and David Hirshey, for guiding us through the journey.

Richard Ljoenes, for the great cover; Margot Schupf, for those extra photos; and Steve Ross, for making things happen in less than 1.2 seconds.

Monsignor Dan Dillabough, for the spiritual guidance.

Bill Fioravanti, for the custom tuxedos that are a perfect fit for the future.

Bally, who's taught us unconditional love.